SAFE
BY DESIGN

SAFE
BY DESIGN

A Behavioral Systems Approach to
Human Performance Improvement

Judy Agnew & David Uhl

Performance Management Publications

Performance Management Publications
3344 Peachtree Road NE, Suite 1050
Atlanta, GA 30326
678.904.6140
www.aubreydaniels.com/store

ISBN: 978-0-937100-30-1

Cover design: Mark Robinson, Sr.

To Aubrey, for your steadfast belief in me and for providing me with a career filled with positive reinforcement. And to Matthew and Kianna for enriching my life in so many ways. What a joy it has been to watch you grow into the intelligent, thoughtful, beautiful, fun, resilient adults you have become.

—Judy

To Aubrey, whose teachings and books introduced me to a field of study (and later to a company) that ultimately became the profession that I love. And to Lisa, Jack, Max and Jameson, for your unwavering love and support while I spent many days away from home over the past couple of decades. Thanks for making it possible for me to do this work and for making all the moments with each of you, upon my return, so fulfilling!

—Dave

PRAISE FOR *SAFE BY DESIGN*

Agnew and Uhl are masters in this space! This book defines the critical system and behavioral components of a highly-functioning safety system, and how to improve them within an organization. This latest book is a great reinforcement for experienced practitioners and a wonderful guide for those new to organizational and behavioral safety. The authors use real examples that demonstrate the power of leadership actions and behaviors for creating a positive work environment and a just culture.

—Susie Scott, Director of Corporate Safety
Delta Air Lines Inc.

This book is an ideal resource for leaders seeking to learn the important skills needed to effectively lead safety. Without an in-depth knowledge of the behavioral principles taught in the book, leaders are likely to repeat the cycle of doing the same things and expecting different results. **Safe by Design** *provides a template for engaging staff to seek solutions that supply the safest care to patients and themselves! There is so much value in this book that will transform the culture of healthcare organizations!*

—Tracy M. Abrams, Chief Nursing Officer
Retired USAF, NC

Safe by Design *is an invaluable read for anyone with a desire to improve performance in the workplace through achieving and maintaining the desired behaviors which move the needle for their organization. Judy and David really hit the mark here simplifying the understanding of how organizational systems influence behavior and showing how to bring about positive performance change in not only safety but any aspect of a business. As a practicing disciple and former student of these folks and their peers at ADI, there is nothing more impactful to bring about improvement, which I have done in my career, than utilize these tools on a daily basis.*

—J.W. (Jim) Latham III, General Manager
Baltimore Marine Terminal
CONSOL Marine Terminals LLC

CONTENTS

Part One: What We Know About Human Performance

Part Two: Using the Science to Improve Systems

Appendix One

Appendix Two

INTRODUCTION TO PART ONE

To understand how systems influence human performance you first need to understand human performance scientifically. The first half of the book provides a foundation by introducing the science of behavior as a systems approach. We start with a discussion of aligning values and leader behavior and then provide an alternative way to think about mistakes and errors in order to avoid blame. Next, we provide an overview of the science and give examples of how systems influence safety-related behaviors in often undesired ways. Part One ends with a discussion of trust as a prerequisite to thorough systems analyses.

CHAPTER 1

ABOUT VALUES

It was the first meeting with a prospect. A large manufacturing company was looking to improve safety. The presenting issues were familiar: a respectable safety record that had improved over the past decade but plateaued over the last few years, frustration with persistent slip, trip and fall incidents and forklift collisions, most of them minor, but with catastrophic potential. What was unique about this meeting was that the head of safety said he knew the solution to the problem; he just didn't know how to make it happen. The key, he said, was for all 80,000 employees to *make safety a personal core value.*

Are Values Enough?

The goal of making safety a personal core value makes sense on the surface. If something is a personal core value, that implies it is of upmost importance and therefore individuals will behave in ways that are consistent with that value. Of course, nothing is ever that simple.

First, it is difficult to define *personal core value.* What does that mean? Does it mean the same thing to everyone? Second, even if we could define it clearly for all to agree, how do you get 80,000 people to adopt safety as a personal core value? Just telling people it is a good idea won't do it. Mandating it won't work either. Third, how would you know if someone had adopted safety as a core value? People might tell you safety is a core value, but self-reporting is notoriously unreliable. The most obvious measure of whether something is a core value is to observe behavior. If someone is kind to others we assume kindness is a core value. If someone is always on time, we assume timeliness is a core value. But even this is unreliable because people do not always behave in ways that are consistent with their values. Most of us would say being healthy is a value and yet many of us behave in ways that are inconsistent with that value by eating unhealthy foods and not exercising enough. Values and behavior do not always match.

This is not to suggest that values are irrelevant. In fact, we believe declaring safety as a value is an important first step. The advantage to starting with values is they are a rare point of agreement within organizations. Everyone agrees that safety is important. Of course, stating safety as a value doesn't automatically translate into improvement. Behaving in ways consistent with our values requires deliberate effort for most people. It requires checking our behavior against our values regularly and adjusting our behavior if needed. For example, if we say timeliness is a value and we are late more than we are on time, then we need to adjust our behavior (e.g., leave earlier, set alarms, etc.) so that we can arrive on time more often. If we state that being healthy is a value then we need to adjust our behavior (e.g., eat more fruit and vegetables and exercise daily). This practice of checking behavior against values and then making adjustments is not something most people do habitually.

Values and behavior do not always match.

For leaders, behaving in ways consistent with the value of safety is even more complex. It requires being able to predict how your behavior as a leader will influence the behavior of others and then checking that impact against your values.

Every leader we have ever worked with values the safety of his/her employees and they often do things with the intention of keeping employees safe. Unfortunately, sometimes those leader actions have a different impact. For example, when a serious incident occurs, a senior leader may choose to discipline the employee and/or the supervisor, thinking that will send a message to others that safety is important. The assumption is that such a message will cause people to work more safely. Regrettably, this is often not the outcome. While hearing about the discipline of others may

Leaders must check how their behavior influences the behavior of others and then check that impact against values.

temporarily improve safe behaviors, it is not likely to last. Furthermore, when negative consequences are used frequently, there are side effects that actually undermine safety, not improve it. The point is it is all too easy for leaders who value the safety of their employees to do things that undermine the safety of those employees.

Values-Behavior-Impact Alignment

So, if leaders value safety and truly want to do the right thing, how can they ensure their actions match their values? They first need to check that their intentions and values are aligned. Next, they need to check the alignment of their intentions with the actual impact of what they do. If they use discipline to discourage particular at-risk behaviors, does that result in fewer instances of those behaviors—not just in the short term but in the long term? They also need to look at the side effects of their actions. Use of negative consequences can result in suppressed reporting, which ultimately undermines safety improvement. Questions to ask include:

- What are the company values around safety?

- What are my personal values around safety?

- What will I do proactively and reactively around safety and what is the intended impact of those actions?

- What is the actual impact of my actions?

- What are the side effects of my actions?

- Does the impact match my intention?

- Does the impact align with my values?

In addition to assessing the effects and side effects of their own actions, leaders also need to assess the impact of the organizational systems they create and maintain. If they value the reporting of hazards, they need to analyze the hazard remediation system. Is it functioning as intended? Are there things that inadvertently discourage reporting of hazards such as delays in hazard remediation, or worse, hazard reports that go unaddressed?

Aligning actions with values is challenging for leaders given all the variables they must consider, and also because it requires being able to accurately analyze and predict behavior. Leaders need to be able to predict how people will behave when interacting with a certain management system. For example, what effect will imposing a quota on safety observations have on observers and on the observed workers? Will it result in increased quality observations or pencil whipped observation forms? This is where the science of behavior becomes invaluable.

This book outlines how to use this science to adjust organizational systems (including management systems) to improve safety performance and safety culture.

CHAPTER 2

ABOUT WORDS: MISTAKES, ERRORS, AND BLAME

We all know that humans make mistakes. Despite this, there is an unacknowledged assumption in many organizations that errorless operation is achievable. While few would publicly declare that perfection is possible, the way many organizations treat people who make mistakes reveals the assumption. When employees are blamed, shamed, and disciplined after incidents and near misses, the implication is they should have been able to perform their work without error.

Fortunately, there are people who have seen the problem with this assumption and have worked to correct it. The commercial nuclear industry has long talked about the importance of accepting the fact that humans are fallible. This quote from the Institute of Nuclear Power Operations (INPO) Human Performance Reference Manual (2006, INPO 06-003) is a succinct summary of their position:

> There is always a chance of error. Humans possess an *innate tendency* to be imprecise—"to err is human." Human nature comprises all mental, emotional, social, physical, and biological characteristics that define human tendencies, capabilities,

and limitations. For instance, humans tend to perform poorly under high stress and time pressure...Error is always a factor to be reckoned with in any human activity. (p. 21).

Their stance is that by acknowledging that people will make mistakes (do things they should not do; fail to do things they should do), organizations can track and then anticipate those mistakes and work to prevent them. They promote the identification of error precursors, which then inform preventative strategies. The nuclear industry is a champion for the idea that any instance of human error (incident, near miss, observed deviation from protocol) is a source of precursor information and therefore an opportunity to learn.

The fact that human error is inevitable and to expect errorless work is irrational has become more mainstream due to the work of James Reason, Sidney Dekker and others in the (HOP) Human and Organizational Performance (aka *Safety Differently* and *Safety II*) Movement. They point out that rather than being viewed as a problem of the individual, human error should be viewed as a symptom of a problem in the system within which people are working. They note that since mistakes are inevitable, the response should not be discipline or other forms of negative consequences. Instead, mistakes should prompt investigations of the organizational systems to identify problems in those systems and correct them. A related and important point embedded in these discussions is the truism that punishing people for making mistakes is not only not helpful; in fact, it is harmful (more about this later).

Another Way of Talking About It

We completely agree with the points outlined above. We suggest, however, that there is another way of talking about this important issue that will better help prevent the blame and punishment that is too often the outcome when things go wrong. Phrases like "mistakes are inevitable," "humans are fallible" and "people make errors" are in themselves problematic because the words "mistake," "fallible" and "error" imply a problem with the performer. Consider, for example, that when most of us make a "mistake" or "error" we feel compelled to apologize for it. There is an assumption of fault. This assumption of fault often leads to blame.

Over 80 years ago, the field of Behavior Analysis pointed out the fallacy of blame when research on behavior clearly pointed to environmental influences. Early behavioral researchers noted that blaming individuals for mistakes is a red herring that distracts from investigating true causes. Decades of behavioral research demonstrates that behavior is a function of individual learning histories and the environment within which behavior occurs. Thus, behavioral scientists and practitioners look for behavioral causes in the relationships between the person and the environment. To clarify, "environment" includes any stimuli present where the behavior occurs. It includes physical (e.g., machines, tools, lighting, temperature), social (e.g., peers, leaders, customers, self) and organizational (e.g., pay systems, scheduling, work procedures, staffing) influences.

Phrases like "mistakes are inevitable," "humans are fallible" and "people make errors" are in themselves problematic.

Talking about behavior as being a function of the environment redirects attention from the individual to the environment. It allows us to avoid talking about a person "making a mistake" and instead talk about environmental events that encouraged and enabled undesired behavior. Behaviorists start with the knowledge that behavior is a function of the environment, and thus look first to the environment, not the individual.

It is worth noting that some in the safety field misunderstand and misrepresent behavioral approaches, claiming that behavioral strategies "blame the worker." This is due to an oversimplified, incomplete or inaccurate understanding of the science of behavior. Ironically, behavioral psychology has asserted and scientifically demonstrated the exact opposite for over 80 years. For a more detailed discussion of this issue see Appendix A: *Is Human and Organizational Performance (HOP) a New Approach to Safety?*

A focus on the environment leads to a more accurate understanding of behavior. We no longer throw up our hands and assume an incident was the fault of a rogue employee who just didn't care, we know to assess the physical and social environment the employee works in to identify variables that enable and encourage the behavior of that individual (and likely others who work in the same environment). This focus helps us avoid placing blame where it doesn't belong—with the individual, rather than with the environment. That is not to say that there is no room for discipline of individual employees. Discipline is sometimes the correct choice.

That said, in our collective 50+ years of working with organizations, we have found that doing a thorough behavior analysis of incidents more often than not points to organizational systems (i.e., the environment) as the primary cause, rather than the individual. In those rare occasions when the analysis demonstrates the organizational systems and management practices were well aligned to support safe behavior and the employee engaged in at-risk behavior anyway, then discipline is called for. Sidney Dekker calls such circumstances "blatant and willful" violations. The issue of when to discipline is discussed in the book *Safe by Accident?* (Agnew & Daniels, 2010). Below is an excerpt. For more detailed information see Appendix B: *Punishing People Who Make Mistakes.*

> *If punishment is to be reserved for blatant and willful violations, how will you decide what is blatant and willful and what is an honest mistake? This will always be a judgment call. In Dekker's words: "To think that there comes a clear, uncontested point at which everybody says, 'Yes, now the line has been crossed; this*

is negligence,' is probably an illusion."[1] Dekker suggests that who draws the line is the critical decision and recommends including "practitioner peer expertise" (peers who do the same work). This is important because, as noted earlier, management and safety personnel (those usually involved in investigations) cannot fully understand the behavioral and physical conditions under which the work is done. A peer can.

In addition, we suggest including an expert in behavior analysis. It is far too easy and too common to conclude that if a person was trained in the safe behavior but did something at-risk instead, that it was willful and blatant. In our experience, when analyzed from a behavioral perspective, many cases of seemingly blatant safety violations can be shown to have systemic, organizational contributors to the behavior.

It is important to point out that a behavioral approach does not eschew accountability. Accountability is essential for improvement, but only if the correct people are held accountable for the appropriate behaviors. Backward-looking, blaming accountability rarely leads to lasting improvement. Instead, we should hold people accountable for forward-looking, preventative actions. Systems are designed and maintained by people. Therefore, there should be accountability for those who control the systems to change the systems if they are faulty. Once the systems are changed then everyone who works in those systems should be held accountable— positively reinforced for engaging in safe behaviors and corrected when they are not. This is not about absolving personal responsibility—quite the opposite. It is about establishing accountability at all levels that will lead to true improvement.[2]

---

[1] Dekker, S. (2007). *Just Culture: Balancing Safety and Accountability.* Ashgate Publishing Limited. Burlington, VT. p. 78.

[2] For more on this subject see Appendix C: *Personal Responsibility Within a Behavioral Approach.*

Aligning Intention with Impact

It is important to note that truly understanding behavior requires assessing the influence of environmental stimuli and events as they actually impact behavior, not as they are intended to impact behavior. Said plainly, the emphasis should be on impact, not intent. Leaders often do a cursory assessment and come to the wrong conclusions. For example, a leader might say, "The equipment has guarding, there are signs posted in the work area, the employees had training, we told them in the weekly meeting they don't need to rush, therefore, the environment was set up to ensure they work safely." While it is true the *intention* was to set them up to work safely, it might not be true that those efforts actually *did* set them up to work safely. Where is the evidence that the actions taken had the intended impact? Furthermore, there are undoubtedly other unidentified variables that influenced behavior in undesired ways. Beyond lengthy observation, the only way to truly understand how environmental events influence behavior is to either ask the performers or (if they are unlikely or unable to report honestly) put yourself in the performers' shoes and assess all possible environmental influences. The science of behavior provides the structure to do this.

Truly understanding behavior requires assessing the influence of environmental stimuli and events as they actually impact behavior, not as they are intended to impact behavior.

For example, a few years ago we helped a large mining organization understand and address an issue they had with adoption of Stop Work Authority. The safety group and senior leaders were frustrated that incidents kept occurring that could have been prevented if employees had stopped work when a safety concern arose. The organization had a big campaign around Stop Work Authority, including clear communication around the circumstances under which it should be used, and the fact that no negative consequences would be associated with stopping work. After doing an analysis that involved putting themselves in the employees' shoes and thinking through all the potential consequences for stopping work (for the performer) it became evident why many employees were reluctant to stop work. Some of the consequences included peer pressure to keep working, incentives for production, individual desire to get the job done and be seen as a good worker, and immediate negative reactions of supervisors to stopping work. After the analysis, the group understood that simply initiating another communication campaign about the importance of stopping work would never solve the problem. The analysis uncovered the true environmental variables that discouraged stopping work, which the team was then able to address. They made adjustments to their incentive system, held micro-training sessions for supervisors and the front line on how to encourage appropriate stop work, and instituted a multi-pronged positive reinforcement process to recognize and further encourage stop work when it occurred.

Near-miss reports, incidents, and deviations from procedures are great learning opportunities, but a superficial understanding of behavior will only muddy the lesson.

In summary, the environment within which people work can and often does encourage at-risk behavior, despite good intentions. The environment includes both formal systems such as incentives and reporting systems and informal systems such as peer pressure and casual communications. Informal systems are not deliberately designed and managed, however, they can have significant impact on behavior. The more leaders and safety professionals can accurately identify both the formal and informal systems and how they influence behavior, the better able they are to make adjustments to the systems in order to increase safe work. Near-miss reports, incidents, and deviations from procedures are great learning opportunities, but a superficial understanding of behavior will only muddy the lesson. Understanding behavior scientifically is key to avoiding blame and ultimately improving safety.

CHAPTER 3

HOW SYSTEMS INFLUENCE WORK BEHAVIOR

We made the case in the first two chapters that learning about the science of behavior is key to improving safety. Dr. Aubrey Daniels and others at ADI have written extensively about the science as it applies to business (see Suggested Readings list in Appendix Two) and we encourage the reader to go beyond this book and learn as much as possible. The more you learn about the science, the more effective you will be. Below is a condensed summary of the scientific findings most relevant for the subject of this book—how organizational systems influence work behavior.

The foundation of the science of behavior is the ABC Model, which illustrates the two influences on behavior: antecedents and consequences.

ANTECEDENT—BEHAVIOR—CONSEQUENCE

Antecedents are anything that come before behavior that prompt behavior. Training, signs, and SOPs are good examples. They are designed to prompt certain safety behaviors. Consequences are anything that come after behavior that influence whether that behavior happens again. The term "consequence" has negative connotations for many, but in the science, consequences can be positive or negative. Positive consequences strengthen behavior and negative consequences weaken behavior. Praise, discipline, discomfort, reduced effort, and incentives are all examples of potential consequences.

While seemingly simple, the ABC Model will profoundly change the way you approach safety once you understand and apply it. Below are some of the most basic, and important contributions the science has made to our understanding of behavior. While most people exposed to these basic concepts quickly acknowledge them to be true, they are only haphazardly applied to the design of most safety management systems. After a brief description of the fundamental concepts, we share how some common safety management practices often fail to account for these scientific findings and are thus less effective.

Antecedents

What the science tells us: Antecedents are anything that comes before behavior that prompts behavior. Research shows that antecedents lead to short-term change in behavior when used alone. Antecedents such as training, procedures, clear instructions, checklists, and safety meetings are important. They inform people what is required and under what conditions. However, even the best training, procedures, and meetings are not sufficient to ensure consistent safe behavior and safety leadership behavior.

BOTTOM LINE
Antecedents are necessary but not sufficient.

Common practices that don't align with science: Safety Management Systems are comprised largely of antecedents. Think of the components of your safety management system and categorize them in terms of antecedents (come before behavior and prompt behavior) or consequences (follow behavior and strengthen or weaken it) and you will see they are disproportionately antecedents—they are intended to set people up to do the right thing. For example: equipment checklists, pre-task risk assessments, leader training on conducting safety interactions, lists of SIF prevention behaviors, cold/hot weather campaigns, and signage. These components alone, no matter how well designed and executed, will not lead to everyone doing the desired behaviors consistently over time.

BOTTOM LINE
Organizations over-rely on antecedent solutions that are destined to have limited impact.

Consequences

What the science tells us: Behavior is strongly influenced by consequences. What happens to us after we engage in a behavior will determine, over time, whether we continue to do that behavior or not. If a behavior leads to quicker completion of a job, perceptibly better work, recognition from leaders, peers or customers, etc., we will keep doing it. If a behavior leads to a delay in completing a job, discomfort, frustration, criticism from peers or leaders, we will likely stop engaging in that behavior.

BOTTOM LINE
Consequences are key to understanding and improving behavior.

Common practices that don't align with science: Despite general understanding that consequences are of upmost importance, most organizations use relatively few consequences for safety. As noted above, if you think about how much time you spend on antecedents relative to consequences, you will quickly see the disconnect. Furthermore, when consequences are used, they are often less effective than leaders realize. There are variables that determine the power of any consequence that are rarely considered when planning consequences (more on this below). Finally, most organizations fail to account for (or dismiss) the natural consequences embedded in the organizational systems (e.g., discomfort, reduced dexterity, difficulty), which all too often encourage and enable at-risk behavior.

BOTTOM LINE
Organizations underuse consequences in general and overestimate the effectiveness of the consequences they do use.

Timing and Probability

What the science tells us: Timing and probability have a tremendous influence on how effective a consequence is. Consequences that occur while the behavior is happening or immediately after, are more powerful than those which occur hours, days, months or years later. Think of this on a continuum. The further away in time, the weaker a consequence gets. Similarly, consequences that are high probability to the performer (more certain) are more powerful than those that are low probability (more uncertain). Again, think of it on a continuum. The more uncertain a consequence is to the performer, the weaker it is. Combining these two variables with whether a consequence is experienced as positive or negative to the performer, makes it possible to predict the impact a consequence is likely to have. Positive or negative consequences that are both immediate and certain are the most powerful. We call such consequences PICs (**P**ositive, **I**mmediate, **C**ertain) and NICs (**N**egative, **I**mmediate, **C**ertain).

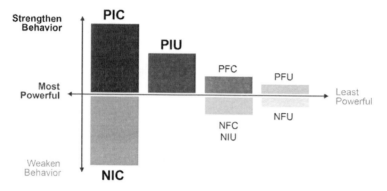

This figure shows the relative power of potential consequences classified through a PIC/NIC Analysis®.

This fact of nature means that seemingly insignificant consequences (saving a few minutes, being more comfortable) can be extremely powerful when they are immediate and certain. Likewise, seemingly significant consequences (getting injured, earning an incentive) can be weak when they are in the future and/or uncertain. This analysis of the timing and probability of a behavior's consequences is an essential component of ADI's PIC/NIC Analysis.®[1] This tool enables an analysis of any behavior in terms of its antecedents, and more importantly, the consequences that influence the behavior. Each consequence is categorized based on whether it is positive or negative to the performer, immediate or future, and certain or uncertain. The PIC/NIC Analysis® not only leads to better understanding of at-risk behavior, but importantly, it leads to more effective solutions that address true causes.

---

[1] For a detailed description of the PIC/NIC Analysis,® see *Performance Management: Changing Behavior that Drives Organizational Effectiveness* (full reference in the Suggested Readings).

BOTTOM LINE
Immediate and certain consequences are
extremely powerful.

Common practices that don't align with science: Most planned organizational consequences are either in the future or uncertain or both. Celebrations based on lack of incidents are a good example. An end-of-the-year celebration for having no lost time incidents is both future and uncertain, and thus in the weakest category.[2] Praise from a manager for an observed safe behavior would be immediate, but in most organizations is highly infrequent (uncertain), thus less powerful. Alternatively, the fact that safety glasses fog up every time a worker puts them on is both immediate and certain. The fact that following a lengthy procedure for locking out and tagging out slows the job down is both immediate and certain. These potential negative, immediate, certain (NIC) consequences serve to decrease the likelihood that workers will engage in the safe behaviors.

BOTTOM LINE
Relying heavily on future and uncertain
consequences is simply not enough to offset the
immediate and certain consequences embedded in
the work environment and organizational systems.

---

[2] There are other problems with linking consequences to periods of time without incidents that are covered in Chapter 8.

NEGATIVE CONSEQUENCES (PUNISHMENT AND NEGATIVE REINFORCEMENT)

Punishment

What the science tells us: A punisher is any consequence that follows behavior that decreases the probability of that behavior. In everyday language, a "punisher" is used to refer to something deliberate and fairly severe (fines, progressive discipline, etc.). In the science, a punisher is anything, big or small, that decreases behavior. As noted earlier, how immediate and certain a punisher is will determine its impact. Discomfort, hassles, restricted freedom of movement, are all examples of potential immediate and certain punishers. In fact, those seemingly small consequences discourage many safe practices. It is important to note, these examples are not intentional punishers, they are embedded in the equipment, procedures, tools, systems, and the work itself.

Negative Reinforcement

What the science tells us: Under negative reinforcement, people engage in behavior to avoid something bad (technically, to avoid a punisher). Negative reinforcement strengthens behavior. We are more likely to do things that help us avoid or escape something unpleasant. Examples include putting on a coat to avoid being cold, setting a reminder to avoid forgetting an important appointment, or driving the speed limit to avoid a ticket when a police car is in sight.

Punishment and negative reinforcement work together; they are flip sides of the same coin. For example, if we drive *over* the speed limit and get a ticket, that is punishment. If we *drive* the speed limit and avoid getting a ticket, that is negative reinforcement. Without the possibility of punishment, there is no negative reinforcement. Negative reinforcement is often established with threats such as, "If you don't lock out and tag out you will get fired." This threat will only work to strengthen the behavior if employees believe they will get fired. We all know "empty threats" don't work.

Negative reinforcement produces a pattern of behavior we call "just enough to get by." People do what they have to do in order to avoid the punisher, but no more. For example, workers may engage in the safe behavior only when a supervisor is present, or only when the perceived risk is very high. Furthermore, if negative reinforcement and punishment are the primary consequences in a workplace, they generate undesirable side effects such as lower trust, reduced engagement, and underreporting.

> ## BOTTOM LINE
> Relying on negative reinforcement and punishment results in just-enough-to-get-by performance and side effects that undermine safety culture.

Common practices that don't align with science: Much of safety is managed via negative reinforcement and punishment. We tell people to follow procedures to avoid getting hurt (negative reinforcement). We establish Lifesaving Rules or Cardinal Rules and state that violations of those rules will result in termination (negative reinforcement of rule-following). If we observe people who aren't following procedures, we reprimand or discipline them (punishment). Negative reinforcement is the default approach to safety management. If nothing else, workers know that if they don't work safely, they may get injured and/or get in trouble. These are ever-present consequences regardless of what other things leaders do. This fact, combined with underutilization of positive reinforcement, results in the manifestation of the side effects which undermine culture. While negative reinforcement and punishment are an inevitable and important part of safety management, they are easily overused.

BOTTOM LINE

Negative reinforcement and punishment are the default approaches to managing safety, and they undermine safety culture.

Positive Reinforcement

What the science tells us: Positive reinforcement is anything that follows behavior that strengthens that behavior. Some examples of potential reinforcers include things that makes the job easier or more comfortable, peer approval, a sense of accomplishment, customer appreciation, getting the job done faster, and supervisor praise. Like all consequences, positive reinforcers are often embedded in organizational systems. Unfortunately, often those embedded reinforcers encourage at-risk behaviors in both frontline and management. However, when deliberately and systematically applied, positive reinforcement strengthens desired, safety-related behaviors and reduces the need for negative consequences. Furthermore, it builds trust, strengthens relationships, and encourages engagement and reporting.

BOTTOM LINE

Positive reinforcement (R+) is the most efficient and effective tool for improving safe behaviors at all levels and is the only consequence that has positive side effects.

Common practices that don't align with science: Positive reinforcement is one of the most misunderstood concepts in business. It is often described as being about making people feel good or acknowledging outstanding performance rather than as a tool to build consistency in behavior at all levels of the organization. For this and other reasons, organizations use more negative than positive consequences, especially for safety. If you ask most frontline employees about the ratio of positive to negative consequences around safety, the vast majority will say they get far more negative ones. A common refrain is, "I only hear from my boss when I have done something wrong." This "safety cop" approach is reflective of the reactive approach so many organizations still take to safety. As noted, organizations also tend to overestimate the impact of the positive consequences they do use, often assuming an annual incentive or monthly safety BBQ offsets daily and weekly negative consequences. They also fail to account for the positive reinforcers embedded in the work processes and organizational systems that often work against safety. A 4:1 ratio (positive to negative consequences) is ideal for maximizing performance and yet in most organizations the ratio is reversed.

BOTTOM LINE
Positive reinforcement is the most underutilized tool for improving safety performance and safety culture.

Sources of Antecedents and Consequences

What the science tells us: The ABC Model is not as simple as it appears. Every behavior has multiple antecedents and consequences that can influence that behavior. The more sources you can identify and manage, the more effectively you can manage behavior. Furthermore, consequences that are embedded in the work environment are often the most immediate and certain and thus most powerful. Failing to account for their influence is to ensure inconsistent safety performance.

BOTTOM LINE
All possible sources of antecedents and consequences should be identified and managed for optimal safety performance.

Common practices that don't align with science: Most organizations fail to recognize all the sources of antecedents and consequences, particularly those embedded in organizational systems and the work itself. Such antecedents and consequences often do not support safe behaviors. Many leaders point only to the antecedents and consequences they have engineered into the systems and are frustrated they are not having the desired impact. For example, when lamenting poor participation in a hazard-reporting program, leaders often point to the strong communications and planned consequences they believe should work better, such as a random drawing for a gift card for all those who report a hazard in a month. What they don't recognize is that reporting a hazard takes time away from work, is a hassle, and those who report often don't hear back about the resolution. Because behavior is multiply-controlled, it is essential to identify all sources of antecedents and consequences, especially the unintended ones. Behavior analyses of systems will help illuminate those sources.

In summary, the science of behavior provides an indispensable framework for identifying and adjusting the variables that influence safety-related behaviors. To be optimally effective, organizations must look beyond the planned antecedents and consequences. In the next chapter, we discuss how to look for and recognize all sources of antecedents and consequences and improve the consistency of safety performance at all levels of the organization.

BOTTOM LINE

Effective safety management must acknowledge and manage antecedents and consequences from all sources, especially those embedded in organizational systems.

CHAPTER 4

GOOD WORKERS IN BAD SYSTEMS

We believe most people want to do a good job and want to work safely. Some might say this is naïve but approaching safety with this perspective tempers the tendency to blame and steers us toward better solutions. Unfortunately, many leaders are still too quick to blame the worker, especially in safety. They are too quick to assume management did all they could, and the workers just messed it up. We should all know better by now, shouldn't we? Consider what a sample of management gurus have said about this matter over decades.

> In the early 1980s quality guru, Edwards Deming, said that over 90% of the problems of quality could be attributed to management, not the front line.[1]

> In the late 1980s Stephen Covey said, "So often the problem is in the system, not in the people."[2]

> In 1995 Geary Rummler and Alan Brache wrote, "If you pit a good performer against a bad system, the system will win almost every time."[3]

---

[1] The W. Edwards Deming Institute. www.deming.org

[2] Covey, Stephen R. *The Seven Habits of Highly Effective People: Restoring the Character Ethic.* New York: Simon and Schuster, 1989.

[3] Rummler, G. A. & Brache, A. P. *Improving Performance: How to Manage the White Space on the Organization Chart.* San Francisco, CA: Jossey-Bass, Inc., (1995), p 13.

In 2005 Aubrey Daniels and James Daniels wrote, "Leaders create the culture, the place, and the conditions for employees and their work. This includes the physical conditions and the management process. The most effective leaders first look at those elements before looking to individuals or groups of employees for assigning blame or attempting a fix. Most failures of organizations are failures of the management process, not employees' behavior."[4]

For over 40 years, management experts have been telling us the equivalent of, "It's the system, stupid."

Below are some recent examples of putting good people in bad systems and then blaming the people when things go wrong. We first describe what traditional incident investigations found. Because these investigations tend to look only at the intended antecedents and consequences, the management responses to the incident may seem reasonable. Rigorous behavior analyses of the same incidents lead to different conclusions. By analyzing all the antecedents and consequences embedded in the operating environment, it becomes clear that in each case, blame and punishment are unjust and unhelpful.

As you review these incidents, keep the following scientific facts in mind:

1. Antecedents only prompt behavior. Without supportive consequences the effect of the antecedent will be short-lived.

2. *Immediate* and *certain* consequences are stronger than consequences that are in the *future*, *uncertain*, or both.

Scenario 1: *A professional delivery driver has multiple incidents of speeding and is formally disciplined.*

---

[4] Daniels, A.C. & Daniels, J.E. (2005). *Measure of a Leader: An Actionable Formula for Legendary Leadership*. Atlanta: Performance Management Publications. p. 95.

The traditional investigation confirmed that the driver had Safe Driver Training and was educated in the dangers of speeding. It also confirmed that the company policy states that speeding will not be tolerated. The investigation concluded that the driver knew how to drive safely and knew what could happen if he sped. Yet he sped anyway. After a prior speeding incident, the driver was brought into the supervisor's office and given a warning. This was intended to be a negative consequence to stop his speeding.

While the organization might have believed it had done everything it could to set drivers up to drive the speed limit, the strategies they used were weak. Their consequence strategy was to punish speeding when they caught it. That's a future and uncertain consequence for speeding. How often had the driver been speeding *before* the warning and *between* the warning and the discipline? Furthermore, the organization was not providing any source of positive reinforcement for the behavior they want (driving at or under the speed limit). They expect it to happen automatically because drivers should "know better," and they dealt with exceptions as they caught them. The traditional investigation conducted the analysis solely from management's perspective without considering the perspective of the driver.

A behavior analysis of the same situation considered the intended and unintended antecedents and consequences that were influencing speeding and driving the speed limit. Although the organization wasn't providing positive consequences for driving the speed limit, it was paying drivers per delivery to encourage timely delivery. This incentive likely inadvertently reinforced speeding. The drivers also received tips from customers for timely deliveries. That's two potential sources of positive reinforcement for speeding, and none for driving the speed limit.

Another contributing factor was a shortage of drivers and higher-than-normal work volume. This put pressure on drivers to deliver quickly to avoid things like backlogs, having to stay late, and negative feedback from their supervisors. In addition, the more speedy the deliveries, the higher their earnings from the organizational incentive and tips. While there was always the threat of a negative consequence if caught speeding, other drivers admitted to speeding and claimed that supervisors knew they were speeding but rarely did anything about it (a future and uncertain consequence, which is very weak). The balance of antecedents and consequences (deliberate and embedded) clearly favor speeding, not driving the speed limit.

Scenario 2: *A recently hired construction worker experiences a hand injury because she put her hand in a known pinch point and gets a written warning.*

The traditional investigation highlighted that the employee watched a training video on preventing hand injures and that the supervisor discussed avoiding pinch points during several pre-shift meetings that the employee attended. The investigation also noted that there were tools that could be used to avoid putting hands in pinch points and that the employee was aware of these tools and knew how to use them. The investigation concluded that the employee was aware of the dangers of putting hands in pinch points, knew how to avoid doing so, but still did it.

Again, the organization believed they did what was necessary to prevent employees from putting hands in pinch points, but their strategies were all antecedents and thus weak. The training video was particularly weak in that it was short and did not exactly match the circumstances the employee found herself in on the job site. Furthermore, there were no positive consequences for using proper tools or negative consequences for putting hands in pinch points other than the uncertain possibility of injury.

A behavior analysis of the same situation uncovered some additional unintended antecedents and some powerful consequences that influenced the behavior. The training video was found to be insufficient and there was no on-the-job training to ensure the employee was clear on what to do on the actual job site. The employee was hired along with many other workers because the company had a large project with a tight timeline. Given those pressures, any on-the-job training she might have received was absent.

While the employee understood she could use a tool rather than put her hand in the pinch point, she could never find those tools when she needed them. When she asked other employees, they said there weren't enough of the tools and they often "went missing." The production pressure associated with the big project meant that using hands instead of searching for the scarce tools would save precious time and increase production. These immediate and certain consequences encouraged using hands rather than tools. While the supervisor's discussion of pinch points in pre-shift meetings was a helpful reminder, the new employee noticed that there was no opportunity to raise concerns or ask questions, and none of the more experienced employees used that opportunity to tell the supervisor about the scarcity of the tools. When she asked one of them after a meeting, he rolled his eyes and said, "We have told the supervisor a hundred times that there aren't enough tools and nothing changes." The employee also noted that experienced employees put their hands in the pinch points and nothing bad happened (i.e., there were no consequence for the at-risk behavior). So, while the company intended to provide tools to avoid the hazard, they failed to ensure enough tools were available and to confirm that workers were using them.

Again, the behavior analysis found that the balance of antecedents and consequences (deliberate and unintentional) favored using hands instead of looking for and using tools to avoid pinch points. To discipline this one worker for a behavior that others also do and is a function of management-controlled circumstances is unjust and won't prevent future injuries. If the at-risk behavior has persisted and is only addressed after someone gets hurt, it fuels the perception among the workforce that management doesn't care about unsafe acts as long as they don't result in an injury.

Scenario 3: *A supervisor was discovered to have put in superficial effort on required safety conversations with direct reports and is denied a promotion.*

The traditional investigation noted that clear expectations had been set for supervisors to have two documented safety conversations each week. The supervisor's manager discussed the safety conversations with him as the program was kicked off to ensure he understood the intent of the program and how to document conversations, and there was opportunity for questions and clarification. It also found that while the supervisor sometimes had legitimate, thorough safety conversations with his direct reports, over a period of months prior to the investigation, many of the documented conversations were very superficial and appeared to be done simply to meet the quota.

The organization believed that because the expectations were clear, there was no excuse for the supervisor to do a poor job of safety conversations. No examination of consequences was conducted, including no acknowledgement of the fact that the supervisor had been doing superficial conversations for months and the manager never provided any feedback on any documentation.

A behavior analysis of the situation revealed antecedents and consequences that had a clear role in encouraging the undesired behavior. While the expectations were clear, there was no training in how to have productive safety conversations. The supervisor was a new, young supervisor and his crew was older, seasoned workers so he was uncomfortable having conversations with them (an immediate, certain consequence). The supervisor reported that the safety conversations he did have were awkward and seemed to have no positive impact on safety. These natural consequences discouraged doing safety conversations. In addition, the measure of the safety conversations was purely quantitative (number of conversations completed per week). There was no measure of the quality of conversations and no follow-up by his manager. This lack of consequences led the supervisor to think that it didn't matter whether he conducted good conversations or not. When short on time, he had brief, superficial conversations and again, received no questions or feedback from his manager. Over time, given this lack of consequences, he found himself doing mostly short, superficial conversations just to meet the quota.

The supervisor provided another reason for his behavior which was related to incentives and production. The organization had management incentives tied to TRIR (nothing tied to completing safety conversations) and incentives for weekly production targets. Since he experienced no positive consequences for safety conversations but he received incentives for production, he chose to spend less time on safety conversations in order to spend more time on production. The analysis also noted that the workload for supervisors was high, including a great deal of paperwork that required hours a day at a computer, making it hard to get out to do safety conversations. So having safety conversations took time away from those other tasks which had immediate and certain consequences associated with them.

The behavior analysis showed lack of training in how to have effective safety conversations, and no support for the supervisor to overcome his discomfort with providing feedback to more seasoned workers. Incentives encouraged a focus on production, not safety, and the workload made it very difficult for supervisors to find the time to do the safety conversations. The quota focused on quantity, not quality and there was no follow-up to reinforce quality conversations. The balance of antecedents and consequences favored short, superficial conversations rather than longer, meaningful ones.

Behavior in Context

In each of these scenarios, the behavior analyses show a much richer picture of the conditions under which these individuals were working and help us see why they did what they did. True understanding requires identifying all potential sources of antecedents and particularly consequences embedded in the work environment. Identifying those consequences that are immediate and certain is particularly important. As noted, many of these consequences are unintentional and their impact on safety-related behaviors is unplanned. This makes them difficult to identify. However, when we take the time to discover and assess all antecedents and consequences, we often understand immediately why at-risk behavior occurred. In fact, it is a common experience after doing such analyses for leaders to admit that they themselves would likely have done the same thing.

True understanding requires identifying all potential sources of antecedents and particularly consequences embedded in the work environment.

This more detailed level of analysis helps avoid blame and reduces the use of negative consequences. Many of the antecedents and consequences embedded in the work environment are immediate and certain, and thus very powerful. Once you understand this it becomes clear how unjust it is to discipline or even reprimand workers for many at-risk behaviors. While negative consequences are sometimes appropriate, often they are not. Before using negative consequences leaders need to conduct systems due diligence. If the systems are found to make working safe difficult or impossible, then focusing on changing the systems will be more effective than the more typical strategies based on blaming the worker.

Common Solutions When an Employee is Blamed

Consider the most common solutions to come out of incident investigations when the problem is viewed as a problem with the employee, as opposed to a problem with the system:

- Training/retraining
- Coaching and counseling
- Threatening and/or disciplining
- Termination

It is easy to see why these "solutions" are ineffective. They don't address the source of the problem. Training or retraining is only helpful if the worker was unaware of or unable to do the safe behavior. That is almost never the case (more about this in Chapter 7). Typically, the safe behavior occurs some of the time, just not all the time. Counseling may be part of the solution, but if the systemic causes are not also addressed it is unlikely to result in permanent change. Threatening and/or disciplining (aka negative reinforcement and punishment), as discussed, have negative side effects that are counterproductive to improving safety culture. Punishing people for things outside of their control angers workers, undermines trust, and stifles engagement. Finally, terminating employees involved in

Punishing people for things outside of their control angers workers, undermines trust, and stifles engagement.

incidents does nothing to fix the circumstances that encouraged the behavior, thus other workers are likely to end up doing the same thing. Terminating people also has a chilling effect on the safety culture, fueling an unwillingness to share and underreporting. While the strategies listed are appropriate under the right circumstances, those circumstances are relatively rare. When these strategies are used under the wrong circumstances, they are ineffective at best and counterproductive at worst.

Blame the System

Alternatively, if we view the problem as a systems problem rather than a problem with the individual, our solutions not only prevent the worker in question from getting hurt, but they also prevent anyone else who works in those circumstances from getting hurt. Systemic solutions lead to systemic prevention. Some examples of such solutions include changes to safety equipment, improvement in on-the-job training, modified management messaging that focuses more on safety, changing safety processes to make them less cumbersome, using leading rather than lagging indicators to manage safety, increasing quality supervisor safety conversations, and increasing the use of positive feedback and reinforcement around safety-critical behaviors. The second half of this book will share more examples of systemic solutions.

The first step to systemic solutions is to perform thorough behavioral assessments, which help identify the biggest opportunities for improvement. Where should you look for some of the embedded antecedents and consequences in the work environment and organizational systems? ADI's DE³ Checklist® provides some structure to begin the analysis.

DE³ CHECKLIST®

This is a tool for building a work environment that aligns with safety values and promotes an engaged, progressive safety culture.

DIRECTION	ENVIRONMENT
☐ Safety vision and values are clearly communicated.	☐ Tools and equipment are in good working condition and readily available.
☐ Policies, procedures, and other safety expectations are clear.	☐ Physical layout of the workspace enables and encourages safe work.
☐ Communications around safety are as frequent as those around productivity.	☐ Processes and procedures are free of unnecessary and/or overly cumbersome steps.
☐ Proactive, preventative behavior expectations are clear for leaders and frontline employees.	☐ Staffing is sufficient to meet production demands without taking safety shortcuts.
☐ Measures, incentives and other goals or initiatives are aligned with or not competing with safety expectations and goals.	☐ Sufficient time is provided to work safely.
	☐ Work conditions are designed to minimize stress, fatigue and distractions.
	☐ Hazards and obstacles to safe work are addressed in a timely manner.

EXPERTISE	ENGAGEMENT
☐ Safety training effectively builds necessary skills to work safely.	☐ Timely and helpful feedback is provided for safety-related behaviors.
☐ Training needs are assessed regularly (including technical skills, people skills, leadership skills).	☐ Critical safety behaviors are consistently positively reinforced.
☐ Employees are trained in and reinforced for hazard recognition and remediation.	☐ Overall, there are more positive than negative consequences for safety-related behaviors.
☐ Employees are trained in and reinforced for stopping work when there is a safety concern.	☐ Peer pressure is monitored to ensure it favors safety.
☐ Leaders are trained in and held accountable for proactive safety leadership activities.	☐ Reinforcement and incentives for behaviors that compete with safety are minimized.
☐ Leaders are trained in analyzing behavior scientifically.	☐ Antecedents and consequences around production are balanced with those for safety.
	☐ Safety is managed with leading metrics that promote preventative behaviors.

This tool will help you begin exploring all influences on work behavior at every level of the organization. Of course, the best way to do these analyses is to involve the workers themselves. Those who work within the system are in the best position to identify what the major influences are. However, there is a catch—getting workers to talk openly and honestly requires trust. As noted, overuse of negative consequences (the default for many organizations) undermines trust and makes honest conversations difficult or impossible. Keep in mind what you are asking people to do is tell you what encourages them to engage in at-risk behavior. That's a big ask. If there is any fear of negative consequences, most workers won't talk. For many organizations, building trust is a prerequisite to this kind of employee engagement. Once trust is built, workers and leaders can work together to design effective solutions that support consistent safe work and consistent safety leadership.[5] In the next chapter, we discuss how to create a culture of trust that enables this kind of joint problem-solving.

Overuse of negative consequences undermines trust and makes honest conversations difficult or impossible.

In summary, behavior analyses of systems lead to more effective safety solutions and reduce the blame and discipline that undermine safety culture. This quote from Deming captures the sentiment perfectly.

> *"The aim of leadership is not merely to find and record failures of men, but to remove the causes of failure: to help people to do a better job with less effort."* [6]

---

[5] See Appendix E: *Why Relationships Matter in Safety.*

[6] The W. Edwards Deming Institute. www.deming.org.

CHAPTER 5

THE ROLE OF TRUST IN SYSTEMS ASSESSMENT

As noted in the last chapter, uncovering and analyzing all the systems that contribute to at-risk behavior is a worthwhile, but challenging endeavor. It requires either being able to analyze the job from the worker's perspective (as outlined in the last chapter), or ideally, asking the workers themselves.[1] Not surprisingly, being able to have honest and productive conversations with workers requires a great deal of trust. Workers must be confident that if they speak openly about variables that influence their safe and at-risk behavior there will be no negative consequences. They also need to believe that such open conversations will lead to improvement. In other words, they need to believe management will follow up.

If you generally have good trust in your organization (or your part of the organization) then you may only need to work on building trust in the context of discussing organizational systems and their influence on safety. Set the stage by establishing some ground rules of anonymity and assurances of no negative consequences for those who participate. Since trust is built through actions, not words, plan to shape trust over successive experiences.

---

[1] See Appendix D: *Taking a Safety Culture Selfie.*

The first discussion should focus on a less-serious safe behavior. Avoid analysis of behaviors related to serious injuries or fatalities (SIF) such as lockout/tagout or fall protection, since failure to fully follow such procedures often results in negative consequences. Instead, ask about what encourages workers to temporarily take their gloves off, or to use the wrong tool for a job. Listen carefully, positively reinforce participation, and most importantly, do your best to take their suggestions and implement them. Then, follow up and ask if it helped. Keep making changes until it does. For the next opportunity, ask about something a little more serious, something with a little more risk. For example, ask about a minor procedure for which employees often skip steps. Ask why the steps are skipped and what gets in the way of following the full procedure. Listen, reinforce participation, and follow up. Gradually increase the seriousness/riskiness of the target behaviors and continue providing lots of positive reinforcement and good follow-through. Once workers have the experience of talking candidly without negative consequences and seeing improvement as a result, they will be more willing to talk.

Since trust is built through actions, not words, plan to shape trust over successive experiences.

If you do not have general trust in your organization, you will need to work on that first. Below are some tips to help you build trust and achieve the level of engagement that will enable thorough systems analyses and frank discussions of effective safety solutions.

1. **Build relationships.** Trust is built in the context of relationships. Start by spending time getting to know the people you hope to engage with. Demonstrate you truly care about them and about their health and safety in particular. Employees

who believe you care are more likely to trust your motives when you ask them to be candid about safety.[2]

2. **Extend trust.** Trust is a two-way street. Actively demonstrate your trust in others. Tell them you trust them. Behave as though you trust them. Assume they are trustworthy until they prove you wrong. If workers believe you trust them to do the right thing, they will trust you when you say there will be no negative consequences for candor.

3. **Admit past mistakes.** Most leaders have the best of intentions but sometimes fall into using negative consequences because they don't know what else to do. If you have historically overused blame and negative consequences, then own up to it. Tell workers that you now understand there were things beyond their control that influenced their behavior and that you want to better understand what those are so you can correct them.

4. **Ask more than you tell.** Too many leaders and safety professionals do too much telling and not enough asking. We have all been in a situation where someone is telling us something we already know, or something we clearly know more about than they do. Those experiences make us wonder if the person doing the talking thinks we don't know or worse, doesn't value what we know. Under those conditions, people are less likely to share openly. When you ask more and tell less you make people feel valued and trusted.

5. **Listen actively.** Regrettably, in the age of omnipresent electronic devices, good listening skills are becoming a lost art. This is unfortunate because sincerely and actively listening is one of the best ways to make people feel respected and trusted. Put down electronic devices, look people in the eye (if that is appropriate in your culture) and listen to what they

---

[2] See Appendix E: *Why Relationships Matter in Safety* for more on building strong working relationships.

say. Demonstrate your understanding by asking on-point questions and paraphrasing key points.

6. **Respond positively to bad news.** One of the primary reasons frontline employees don't trust management is that they too often experience (or see others experience) negative consequences after incidents and near misses. Unfortunately, it is easy for leaders to inadvertently discourage reporting of minor incidents and near misses by how they react (more about this in Chapter 9). If you want people to report then you must positively reinforce reporting. To be clear, we are not suggesting positively reinforcing incidents, near misses, or unsafe actions. We are suggesting positive reinforcement for the honest and immediate reporting of those events.

7. **Use more positive than negative.** Positive reinforcement builds trust; negative reinforcement undermines trust. Since most people work safely the majority of the time, they should experience more positive than negative, but the opposite is often the case. Good workers who only hear about safety on the rare occasion when they do something wrong often don't trust that management knows what is really going on. When leaders change their focus to what people are doing well and purposefully recognize the behaviors they want more of, they strengthen those behaviors, and at the same time build relationships and trust.

8. **Do what you say you will do.** This is the ultimate way to build trust. If people open up and tell you about systems and processes that encourage at-risk behavior and you commit to making some changes, then do it or explain why you cannot. This is the best way to build trust over time and encourage more open and honest conversations. But it requires vigilance to follow through, no matter how small the task. Trust is built every time a leader does what s/he says s/he will do. Trust is eroded every time a leader fails to do what s/he says s/he will do.

Creating sustainable safety improvement requires leaders make it okay for workers to tell the truth about how organizational systems (including management practices) influence safe work. Learning and prevention requires open and honest conversations that uncover the unintended antecedents and consequences that prevent hazard identification and remediation and enable at-risk behavior. Too often the overuse of negative consequences has undermined engagement and alienated the people who best know how to improve safety—the frontline workers. But changes in management behavior can turn this around. If leaders become trusted partners with frontline workers and focus their attention on systemic causes and systemic solutions, significant improvement is possible.

Too often the overuse of negative consequences has undermined engagement and alienated the people who best know how to improve safety—the frontline workers.

INTRODUCTION TO PART TWO

The second half of this book will explore the application of the science of behavior to some common safety systems. We have not covered all safety systems. We included what we consider to be some of the more important ones, and the ones most improved by the application of behavioral science.

In each case we start with a scenario, based on our experiences with hundreds of organizations, that exemplifies a safety system that is not working as intended. We then use the science to explain why the system isn't working and provide suggestions for improvement.

In our work doing safety culture assessments, safety leadership training, and coaching, we have seen and helped develop many best practices around safety systems. We have shared some of these to illustrate our points and help the reader with their own applications. We hope that the breadth of systems covered, and the examples provided, will enable the reader to generalize beyond the systems we cover. Once you begin analyzing behavior scientifically, you will begin seeing improvement opportunities, within and outside of safety.

CHAPTER 6

MEASUREMENT SYSTEMS

Hank was a character. He had been with the construction company we were consulting with for 30 years. To say he was "old school" would be an understatement. He worked his way up from journeyman to supervisor and had been in that role for many years. It was clear that Hank was a valued member of the organization. He was the "go-to" guy who always got the job done no matter what the obstacles. He worked hard and expected the same from his crews. While management relied heavily on Hank to get important jobs done on time and on budget, his safety performance was less than stellar. It wasn't that he had a lot of incidents on his jobs; in fact, he had very few. But the safety department complained that getting Hank to participate in safety initiatives was like pulling teeth.

Just prior to our consulting engagement with the company, a relatively new worker on Hank's crew was almost killed in a trenching incident. The investigation revealed that Hank referred to the trenching SOP in the pre-task meeting but did not do a full review of the procedure, nor did he conduct the required verification during the job. When interviewed, the employee stated it was his first time doing this kind of trenching work and was somewhat confused about the safety protocols.

Reading this summary, it is easy to think that Hank bears a good deal of responsibility for this incident. Those who look to blame would likely point the finger at Hank. Indeed, Hank failed to do some things he should have done. But just as we need to take a systems approach to understanding and changing behavior at the front line, we need to look at the systems within which managers and supervisors are working, to understand why they are not more effectively managing safety.

The Importance of the Metric

The system with perhaps the greatest influence on management behavior is the measurement system. How safety is measured significantly influences how safety is managed. The most common are lagging metrics, such as Total Recordable Incident Rate (TRIR),[1] Days Away Restricted, or Transferred (DART), and Workers' Compensation costs. Such metrics tell organizations how many people got hurt and how badly, but they say little about what leaders are doing to prevent incidents. Furthermore, these metrics can be misleading. A company site or department can go months or years without a lost time injury despite poor safety leadership practices.[2] Not every hazard or at-risk behavior (of a leader or worker) turns

How safety is measured significantly influences how safety is managed.

into an incident. As the swiss cheese model illustrates, holes in all of the safety controls need to line up in order for an incident to occur. If organizations don't track and purposefully manage those controls, they end up inadvertently relying too heavily on luck to keep workers safe. Most safety professionals understand this, but some senior leaders do not. Too many senior leaders

---

[1] We recommend reading "The Statistical Invalidity of TRIR as a Measure of Safety Performance" published in *Professional Safety*. See the full reference in Suggested Readings.

[2] Deepwater Horizon is perhaps the most notorious example. They were celebrating seven years without a lost time incident on the day of the explosion.

view lagging safety metrics as more reliable than they are. Unlike production metrics (e.g., pounds of product produced, number of units shipped), which accurately represent the amount of work completed, the number of incidents does not necessarily accurately reflect the safety of an organization. It is a statistical fact that if it were possible to hold all safety activities constant, an organization could experience a different number of incidents from one year to the next. There is simply more variability in safety than in production because we typically don't have tight controls in place. Despite this fact, many senior leaders treat lagging safety metrics as though they are as reliable and predictive as production metrics. This false impression feeds resistance to adopting leading metrics. If the metric is assumed to be working fine, there is no motivation to change it.

It is a statistical fact that if it were possible to hold all safety activities constant, an organization could experience a different number of incidents from one year to the next.

There are other factors that contribute to the reluctance to adopt more leading than lagging indicators, including the fact that lagging metrics are required by regulators and there is a lack of standardized leading safety metrics. As a result, many organizations take the path of least resistance and continue to use lagging safety metrics. Unfortunately, such inaction perpetuates the use of insidious management practices and organizational systems that undermine safety improvement. Consider the following obstacles to safety excellence that are rooted in lagging safety metrics.

Reactive Safety Management—Lagging metrics inadvertently encourage a reactive approach to safety management, in which leaders primarily engage in safety activities after an incident or near miss. As is often noted, this is akin to driving a car by looking in the rear-view mirror.

Prevention Procrastination—During periods of no incidents, when the safety metrics look good, it is easy for leaders to put off preventative safety activities in favor of more pressing non-safety work.

Accountability Misalignment—While most organizations consider safety of primary importance, lagging safety metrics struggle to compete with more frequent, proactive, and reliable metrics for productivity, quality, on-time performance, etc. Naturally, managers will focus on activities for which there are frequent metrics and daily accountabilities. Thus, while safety is stated to be of primary importance, it gets less management attention than other business objectives.

Overuse of Negative Consequences—Measuring what went wrong (incidents) leads to overuse of negative consequences. A change in the numbers means an incident occurred and at that point negative consequences seem most appropriate. It is difficult to use positive consequences after someone has been hurt. Organizations try to offset this trend by celebrating periods of time without incidents, but that strategy is problematic (see below).

Incentivizing the Wrong Behaviors—Most safety incentives are based on lagging indicators, more specifically, going for periods of time without an incident. But what behaviors do such incentives motivate? The hope is they motivate the front line to consistently work safely and leaders to consistently engage in safety leadership behaviors. Unfortunately, there are two other possibilities: (1) safety behaviors are inconsistent, but luck prevails, and no incidents occur, or (2) incidents occur but are not reported. Knowing which of these your incentive is motivating is difficult (and in truth it is often a combination of all three).

Skip-Level Safety Management—Without measures of preventative leadership behaviors, managers of managers have little to talk to direct reports about on a daily and weekly basis. As a result, they tend to focus their safety efforts on frontline employees (doing safety tours, conducting frontline safety interactions, attending toolbox talks, etc.). While these activities can be helpful, they do nothing to build safety leadership effectiveness. By identifying and measuring safety leadership behaviors, managers can actively manage leadership improvement in their direct reports. This kind of cascaded coaching has a multiplicative effect. If a middle manager provides feedback to one frontline employee, only that employee is impacted. If a manager instead spends that time coaching a supervisor in how to more effectively provide feedback to others, that supervisor will go on to influence a whole crew of employees. Improving every supervisor and manager's ability to effectively manage safety is the best path to sustained safety performance.

How Metrics Influenced Hank's Behavior

It is hard to overstate the influence of lagging metrics. They are the foundation of so many of the systems that influence safety behaviors at all levels of the organization, but particularly in leadership. Returning to the case study, let's look at the role metrics played in the incident on Hank's worksite.

The company's primary safety metric was TRIR. They had a management incentive based 40% on production (measured daily and weekly based on project plan milestones), 40% on quality (measured bi-weekly based on quality inspections), and 20% on safety (measured by TRIR). Hank's boss talked to him daily about productivity, and at least weekly about quality. They discussed safety only when there was an issue. Hank was given a lot of positive reinforcement for consistently meeting the project milestones and quality metrics. Leadership made a point to ensure Hank knew he was the "go-to" guy for important and/or difficult projects. He was a good worker and they wanted to keep him around. Hank's boss and others were aware he resisted proactive safety initiatives and activities but because they put him on the tough jobs and expected results, they didn't ride him for safety. When pressed by the safety department, leadership pointed out that Hank rarely had incidents on his projects. Some in the safety department expressed concern about potential underreporting on Hank's jobs but leaders didn't pursue it because they knew Hank truly cared about his crews and wouldn't want anyone to get hurt.

Given the incident occurred just prior to our starting work with the company, we were able to help them do a behavior analysis of the situation. The analysis helped illuminate why Hank did what he did, and most importantly, led to a more effective response to the incident, helping ensure it didn't happen again. In this case, the company's focus on a lagging metric (TRIR) influenced the following:

- The conversations Hank had with his boss were disproportionately about productivity, and to a lesser extent, quality. Productivity and quality were measured more frequently and thus gave the boss something to ask about each day. Unless there was a recordable incident, the safety metric didn't prompt discussions about safety. Leadership was sending an inadvertent message about priorities when productivity was discussed daily and safety only occasionally.

- The incentives (for both Hank and his boss), encouraged both to focus more on production and quality, regardless of how important they considered safety to be. Since Hank had a history of few incidents, the best levers to influence the incentive payout were productivity and quality.

- In addition to incentives, Hank received a good deal of social positive reinforcement for being the "go-to" guy and getting the work done no matter what the obstacles. When he brought a project in on time and on budget, no one asked about safety. They just praised him for getting it done.

- It was easy for leaders to assume Hank was doing a good job of managing safety because he rarely had incidents. This is a dangerous assumption, since we know that a lack of incidents can be a function of luck and/or underreporting, not necessarily good safety management.

- It was also easy for Hank to assume he was doing a good job of managing safety, and thus feel justified in resisting safety initiatives that took time away from production.

- Senior leaders knew Hank wasn't consistently engaging in the proactive safety initiatives promoted by the safety department, but his safety numbers looked good and they wanted to keep him happy, so they didn't provide any constructive feedback or demand change. Hank knew there wouldn't be negative consequences for ignoring the safety initiatives, so he wasn't motivated to change.

Given all these behavioral influences which have foundations in the TRIR metric, it is no surprise Hank didn't pay more attention to safety. It is a scientific fact that we do what we get reinforced for doing. Hank got reinforced for production and quality. His experience was that safety took care of itself, either by employees who did the right things even in the absence of good safety management, or by luck or underreporting (or a combination of all three). It is not that Hank didn't care about safety. The systems he was working within did not encourage daily, proactive safety management activities. Occasional reprimands for not doing more around safety were never going to change anything. Nor would blaming him for the recent incident. Instead, the organization made changes to how they measured and managed safety leadership.

Leading Indicators

When organizations identify and measure the preventative activities required to improve safety, they can then hold supervisors and managers accountable for those activities and strike a better balance between safety and productivity. Leading indicators enable the kind of proactive safety management that is required for sustained safety performance. The million-dollar question is: What are the best leading indicators? Unlike lagging metrics, there is no standard set. Each organization needs to identify metrics that work the best for them. This starts with identifying the preventative activities that will have the biggest impact on safety. These will vary from organization to organization and may change from year to year as safety improves. Keep in mind, there is no perfect leading metric, just like there is no perfect lagging metric. Instead, establish a dashboard or composite index. Continuous analysis and flexibility are key. Take time to assess how the metrics are working to drive the activities you want and whether those activities impact incidents and near misses over time. Plan for a period of assessing and adjusting before linking metrics to financial consequences. Below are some examples of leading indicators to help you start thinking about what will work for your organization.

Leading indicators enable the kind of proactive safety management that is required for sustained safety performance.

Hazard Remediation. Tracking the reporting, and more importantly the remediation of hazards, is a good leading indicator. Obviously, the more hazards that are identified and removed, the safer the workplace, but it is also a measure of engagement and trust.

Near-Miss Reporting. The number of near-miss reports completed is a common and impactful leading indicator. Don't be overly concerned about the volume of seemingly trivial near-miss reports, as long as some proportion is significant. It is a worthwhile endeavor and quality can be shaped over time.

Corrective Actions. Whether from near-miss reporting, hazard identification, audits, safety meetings, or all of these, tracking the percent of corrective actions that have been completed within a certain time frame builds accountability for follow-up. Failure to follow up on corrective actions is a common cause of recurring safety issues.

Behavior-Based Safety. If you have a BBS process, impact metrics such as percent improvement for targeted safe behaviors and improvements in leadership behaviors will enable accountability. Avoid using less important metrics such as number of observations. Such counts of behavior often lead to pencil whipping and do nothing to tell you if your process is working well.

Pre-Task Risk Assessments. If you require risk assessments prior to certain tasks, establish a metric that enables you to determine the quality of those assessments and ideally the impact on behavior. As noted above, simply tracking how many were completed won't necessarily lead to improvement.

SIF Prevention. Many high-hazard industries have identified protocols to prevent serious injuries and fatalities. Adherence to such protocols and follow through on corrective actions associated with the protocols are important leading indicators. SIF exposure rate,[3] while technically a lagging indicator, is helpful at increasing the visibility of SIF events and thus prompting preventative activities.

Supervisor Safety Interactions. One of the most vital behaviors for frontline supervisors is daily safety interactions with workers. Again, don't just track the number of interactions. Develop a metric to assess the quality of the interactions and/or workers' perceptions of effectiveness.

---

[3] SIF exposure rate is a variation of incidence rate that counts serious injuries, fatalities, and injuries that could easily have been more serious or fatal, as well as SIF near misses as the event count divided by person-hours worked.

Safety Leadership Surveys. Surveys can provide timely feedback to leaders on how their actions are supporting and promoting safety. By creating questions that assess agreed-upon leader behaviors (e.g., quality safety interactions, timely follow through on reported hazards), survey feedback can help leaders make specific changes to improve performance.

While the development and ongoing use of leading indicators is more labor intensive than traditional lagging metrics, the effort is essential in order to move beyond the safety plateau that so many organizations experience. Just as the quality movement helped us evolve from measuring quality by the number of customer complaints to sophisticated metrics that enable on-going quality checks and improvements, metrics that enable proactive and positive accountability for prevention will take safety performance to the next level. This requires more effort (as did the quality improvements), but any kind of improvement always does.

CHAPTER 7

TRAINING

It was one of the most interesting assessments we have ever done. The organization was impressive. They were disciplined about safety, very progressive in their approach, and safety was integrated into every aspect of the business. As with many high-performing companies, they were always striving to get better so they asked ADI to do a behavioral assessment of their safety management system. One component of our assessments is a review of root cause analyses completed on incidents and near misses. We look for evidence of systems thinking in their analyses and look at how behavioral problems are analyzed and dealt with. Their root cause analyses were extremely thorough. They looked at systemic causes, including management actions that might have contributed to incidents. While the root cause analyses were progressive, our review of the corrective actions found that 75% were antecedents. Retraining was at the top of the list. The others, while not called "training" were variations of it: reminding employees of procedures, having specific meetings to review safe behaviors, etc. Some version of retraining was their number one solution to the behavioral contributors to incidents.

What was surprising to us was not that retraining was the most common corrective action. This is true in almost every organization we consult with. What was surprising was that this was a company in an industry known for being leaders in safety. Even this very sophisticated company fell into what our colleague Dr. Cloyd Hyten calls the Training Trap.[1]

The Training Trap

Organizations fall into the Training Trap when they assume training will fix most behavioral problems. It is predicated on the assumption that most failures to engage in safety-critical behavior are a function of knowledge or skill deficits. It is a trap because the underlying assumption is not accurate. Rummler and Brache state that only 15-20% of behavioral improvement opportunities fall in the "skills and knowledge" area.[2] This is consistent with our experience at ADI. So, if skills and knowledge are the problem 20% of the time, training should be the solution 20% of the time, not 75%. Why the disconnect? To a large extent it comes back to a lack of scientific understanding of behavior. If you believe antecedents (like training) will result in permanent behavior change then training looks like a good solution. It is also a function of not knowing a better way to address behavior problems.

Avoiding the training trap requires determining whether training is the appropriate solution. Mager and Pipe[3] came up with a simple test to determine whether the performer knew what to do and had the skills to do it: the "Can't Do/Won't Do" test. If the performer cannot do the behavior or task if they really have to, then it's a can't do problem and training is the correct solution. If the performer can do the behavior or task, but they don't, then it is a motivation, barrier, or resource problem, and training is unlikely to help.

[1] Hyten, C., "How to Avoid the Training Trap." *Presentation at ASSE Region III Professional Development Conference.* September 2017, Houston, TX.

[2] Rummler, G. A. & Brache, A. P. (1995). *Improving Performance: How to Manage the White Space on the Organization Chart.* San Francisco, CA: Jossey-Bass, Inc.

[3] Mager, R.F. & Pipe, P. (1999). *Analyzing Performance Problems or You Really Oughta Wanna.* Belmont, CA: Fearon-Pitman Publishers, Inc.

Most incident investigations we have seen do not use this simple test. Instead, when behavior is identified as one of the root causes, retraining is offered as the solution with little attention to whether it will solve the problem and with little attention to the systems within which the behavior occurred. There are many variables (beyond knowledge and skill) that contribute to at-risk behavior such as:

- Unclear or outdated SOPs
- Shortcuts that are consciously or unconsciously accepted by peers and management
- Limited availability of tools
- Equipment in poor condition
- Understaffing
- Production pressure
- Peer pressure

To retrain someone and send them back into an unchanged work environment and expect permanent change is folly. Training will not correct a problem that is a function of organizational systems. As noted in Chapter 4, integrating behavior analyses into investigations helps illuminate the variables behind the "won't do" and leads to developing more effective solutions that target the true causes of at-risk behavior.

To retrain someone and send them back into an unchanged work environment and expect permanent change is folly.

When Training is Appropriate

To be clear, safety training is critically important under the correct circumstances. Workers need to know how to perform their jobs safely, so training is needed for new hires and when there are changes to procedures, equipment, etc. But remember, training is an antecedent, which means it is necessary, but not sufficient. Even the best training is unlikely to result in safe habits without follow-up. We have all had the experience of attending excellent training, being motivated to follow through, but noticing that a month or so later we are back to our old habits. Experience and scientific research prove that training alone simply isn't enough. When training is paired with both on-the-job follow-up to reinforce what was learned and changes in organizational systems to support trained behavior, then sustained behavior change is possible.

While follow-up after training is vital, the quality of the training is also important. Ironically, while organizations over-rely on training, they are simultaneously undermining the effectiveness of the training they conduct. Increased use of poorly designed computer-based training is just one example. Another troubling trend is the breakdown of on-the-job training as organizations get leaner. We too often hear about new employees working independently with very little or no on-the-job training because trainers are stretched too thin. Similarly, good intentions to pair new employees with seasoned employees often fall by the wayside when production demands require using seasoned employees to get the work done. Less experienced employees end up mentoring new employees which can sometimes become a case of the blind leading the blind. None of this bodes well for safety.

Making Training Effective

Once you have determined that training is indeed called for, here are some tips to improve its effectiveness:

- The goal of safety training should always be fluency. Fluency means the performer can complete the task accurately at the optimal speed required for the task. Fluency ensures behaviors persist in the face of distractions. Very few organizational training programs train to fluency. Part of the science of behavior is devoted to how to develop fluency via training. See Appendix G: *New-Hire Training*, for a demonstration of the effectiveness of fluency training.

- While classroom training has its place, some on-the-job training or at least on-the-job verification of skills is essential. As we have been arguing throughout this book, behavior is best understood and managed when looked at in context. Being able to work safely with all the distractions of the actual work environment is the ultimate goal.

- Ensure those doing the on-the-job training themselves have safe habits around critical safe behaviors. This is not always the case. Peers often teach each other shortcuts that improve efficiency without being aware of the risks those shortcuts create. In addition, instruct those doing on-the-job training to aim for fluency. Having a new employee do a behavior correctly once does not mean it is a habit. Repetition under differing circumstances is key.

- Create a follow-up plan that provides feedback and reinforcement for key behaviors over time to ensure the behaviors persist. The follow-up should also provide workers the opportunity to share barriers that get in the way of working safely so that continuous improvement of physical conditions and organizational systems is guaranteed.

Much time and money is spent on safety training and retraining. Using the science of behavior to improve required training will cut down on the need for retraining. In addition, use of the "Can't Do/Won't Do" test will prevent wasting time and money on training solutions that are doomed to fail. Those resources can then be redirected to develop more effective solutions to behavioral challenges.

CHAPTER 8

INCENTIVES

The leadership team was frustrated. For five years they had been actively working on safety, but improvement had stalled. They had a good hazard identification process, their classroom and on-the-job training was effective, and near-miss reporting was increasing. They had a skilled and educated workforce that seemed engaged in safety due, in part, to a popular safety incentive system. The quarterly payout was contingent on no recordable incidents for that period. While incidents were fairly rare, leaders and safety personnel continued to see recurring at-risk behavior and near-miss reports around forklift operations. They knew it was just a matter of time before an incident occurred. Nothing they tried seemed to solve the problem, so they called ADI. We started with an assessment, and the outcome of that assessment was unwelcome news. Among other findings, we reported that their incentive system, while popular, wasn't motivating safe behaviors as intended. Even worse, the incentive was causing underreporting. When we presented our findings, the leadership team refused to believe it. They argued that their frontline workforce were thoughtful people who clearly cared about safety. Those same people, they claimed, wouldn't cover up incidents.

Incentives are one of the most obvious organizational systems that influence safety. The nature of that influence is a source of debate.

Some argue that safety incentives elevate the importance of safety and lead to improvement. Others argue incentives are detrimental to safety. Sorting out the truth requires first clarifying terms. The term "incentive system" covers a wide range of strategies, so it is important to describe the details of the system, in particular, what the payout is based on. In this chapter we will discuss incentives that pay out contingent on lack of (or reduction in) incidents. We will cover common frontline incentive programs (like the one in the scenario above) and common management incentive programs (like the scenario in Chapter 6).

Frontline Incentives

All incentive systems are implemented with good intentions—to reduce or eliminate injury and illness. Unfortunately, as the scenario above illustrates, the actual impact of such incentives is often not the intended one. In our experience, frontline safety incentives based on a lack of incidents do more harm than good. The reason lies in the fact that incentives can be earned for the wrong behavior. As noted in Chapter 6, there are three possible ways to go for a period of time without an incident:

1. Everyone works safely during the entire period. This is what the incentive is designed to motivate—engaging in safe behavior consistently.

2. Workers engage in some at-risk behavior but are lucky in that those behaviors do not result in an incident.

3. Workers don't report incidents that occur during the period.

In this chapter's client scenario, all three ways were undoubtedly involved. The workforce was concerned about safety, genuinely wanted to do the right thing, and often did. However, the leadership team observed recurring at-risk behaviors during forklift use, so clearly the incentive wasn't effective for all safe behaviors. There was also undoubtedly luck involved since the at-risk behaviors had resulted in some near misses, but no injuries to that point. Finally, as confirmed by frontline employees, there was underreporting. As one employee stated, "We are all pretty honest people, but how would you like to be the one to ruin the incentive for the whole team?" She was acknowledging the underlying peer pressure to not report when payouts are linked to group outcomes. Sometimes this peer pressure is blatant (we have heard of employees being physically threatened if they report an incident that results in everyone losing the incentive money), and sometimes it is self-imposed (as in the case above where individuals don't want to be the one to ruin it for others). It is important to note that the greater the incentive the higher the temptation to not report. In this case the payout was $500 per person per quarter.

The injury-based incentive systems we have come across in our work all have similar fatal flaws. At best they reward luck; at worst they reinforce covering up incidents. So why do some organizations continue to use them? One reason is that they can be correlated with a reduction in incidents. As noted, some reduction may be legitimate improvement, but some is likely a function of underreporting. Another reason organizations use such incentives is that employees like them. However, it is important not to confuse what people like with what works. Everyone likes money, but that doesn't mean monetary incentives necessarily result in consistent safe behavior.

Employees like incentives, but it is important not to confuse what people like with what works.

Management Incentives

As with frontline incentives, management safety incentives are implemented with good intentions. The goal is to encourage managers to focus on eliminating incidents. Management incentives are most often part of a broader incentive system including other key performance indicators (KPIs) such as productivity, quality, waste, and customer service. Including safety is a way to indicate the importance of safety and ideally discourage managers from working to improve productivity (or other KPIs) at the expense of safety.

As discussed in Chapter 6, when management incentives are contingent on lagging safety metrics (some form of incident rate), they can inadvertently encourage some undesirable behavior on the part of leaders. When incident rate is low or zero, it is easy for leaders to put safety on the "back burner" and pay more attention to other KPIs such as production and quality. Unfortunately, there is often inadvertent reinforcement for doing so, since failure to proactively engage in safety leadership behaviors for a week or a month is unlikely to result in an incident (or at least to be identified as the direct cause of any incident that does occur). There usually isn't an immediate and direct link between proactive safety management and incidents. Conversely, if metrics for production, quality, customer service, etc. are more sensitive—that is, more directly tied to management behavior—then leaders are more likely to focus on those rather than safety as a way to maximize incentive payout.

Management incentives can also encourage underreporting. We have seen instances where employees don't report incidents because they know that reporting will result in their boss losing incentive money. We have also seen leaders get overly creative to avoid categorizing an incident as reportable so that their incentive payout isn't lost.

Another potential downside of injury-based safety incentives is that they can result in managers spending disproportionate amounts of time attempting to minimize high frequency, low severity injuries (e.g., minor cuts, strains and sprains) at the expense of low frequency, high severity injuries (fall from heights, electrocution). If strains and sprains are preventing payout then that is what leaders will focus on, as opposed to focusing on preventing a serious injury or fatality, since these are rare.

The Dangers of Underreporting

While there are several problems with safety incentives, the most concerning is underreporting. It is impossible to achieve world-class safety performance if your organization is underreporting. Every incident, while unfortunate, is an opportunity to learn, improve, and prevent. As organizations get better and better at safety, those learning opportunities decrease. Of course, that is a good thing because it means fewer people are getting hurt, but it also means the learning slows down. Anything that further limits learning opportunities is to be avoided. Injury-based incentives do just that.

Every incident, while unfortunate, is an opportunity to learn, improve, and prevent.

Link Incentives to Behavior, not Outcomes

Many organizations have experienced the problems with injury-based incentives and have pivoted to incentives based on behavior. In general, this is a better approach. For example, it is better to have frontline incentives that encourage reporting near misses, identifying hazardous conditions, or doing safety observations. Similarly, it's better for management incentives to be based on holding quality pre-shift meetings, timely elimination of hazards, and having quality safety interactions with the front line. Incentives based on preventative behaviors are far more likely to lead to legitimate and sustainable improvements in safety.

While behavior-based incentives are preferable to injury-based incentives, it is important to understand that there is no perfect incentive. Any incentive system can be gamed. Whenever tangible rewards are involved, there is a risk that people will lie or cheat to get the incentives. The larger the incentive, the more likely this will happen.

Unlike tangible rewards (like money), social reinforcement can be delivered more immediately and more frequently, which makes it more effective. Increasing the frequent use of social reinforcement for preventative behaviors will lead to more of those behaviors. When preventative behaviors increase, incident rate takes care of itself. The remaining chapters include examples of social reinforcement for preventative behaviors.

In summary, incentives systems should be carefully reviewed to ensure they are incentivizing the right behaviors. If incentives can be earned through luck or underreporting, they are undermining your ability to achieve world-class safety. Incentive resources are better spent on more effective efforts such as improving hazard identification and remediation, increasing near-miss reporting, and improving safety leadership skills.

CHAPTER 9

NEAR-MISS REPORTING

A young petroleum engineer responsible for a natural gas drilling operation had recently submitted a near-miss report. His company had made significant inroads in establishing "Safety as its Number 1 Value" and as part of that had been emphasizing its near-miss program. Almost immediately after hitting "send" on the electronic report, he received a call from his boss about the near miss. Very soon thereafter, he received a call from his boss's boss. Not too long after that, the VP of his area called to discuss his reported near miss.

He was surprised by the number of inquiries and mildly irritated at having to tell the story repeatedly, but after a few days the calls stopped. The following week he traveled to corporate headquarters for a meeting. When he visited the men's restroom, he found a one-page summary of his near miss posted on the wall. While it did not name any employees involved, there was a photo of what was clearly his drilling rig, up for everyone to see. He thought to himself, "The higher-ups use this restroom, and they're going know that's my rig!" He was embarrassed at the public posting and concerned about his reputation and that of his crew. Despite his commitment to safety, his experience made him question whether or not he would be willing to report another near miss.

Near-miss reporting systems are a great case study for contrasting intention with impact. The intention of near-miss reporting is to promote learning and prevention. As such, more is better. The more near misses reported, the more robust the learning and the better the prevention. However, many near-miss reporting systems actually discourage reporting. When the organization responds in ways that are almost indistinguishable from responses to incidents, the inadvertent message is, "Less is better."

How can organizations avoid inadvertently discouraging reporting and maximize the benefit of near-miss reporting systems? Below are five strategies based on the science of behavior.

Clarify the Intent

While many people appreciate the intent of near-miss reporting, it can be helpful to explicitly promote the rationale. Few would argue with the objectives of organizational learning and incident prevention. However, some may start to waffle when you take the next step and say that more near-miss reporting is better. For those familiar with the traditional safety pyramid, near misses feed into minor incidents or first aid cases, neither of which is good. On a purely optical level, if the goal is fewer recordables and severe injuries at the top of the

When it comes to near misses, more is better.

pyramid, then the goal must be fewer near misses at the bottom of the pyramid. Help discourage this thinking by emphasizing the intent of learning and prevention, which then makes the case that more reporting provides more opportunity to learn and prevent.

Make it as Easy as Possible

In the early days of smart phones we learned the phrase, "There's an app for that!" It is a reference to the fact that someone had figured out a way to make a routine task very simple and easy. Use that mindset with your near-miss reporting system and make it as simple and easy as possible for anyone to report. Several clients have used simple paper forms readily available in break rooms throughout a facility to prompt more reporting. If in-person reporting to a supervisor makes it less likely people will contribute, then allow for employees to report anonymously and/or remotely. If part of your process involves interviewing the reporting party, then make sure they only have to do it once. One of the most common reasons employees give for not reporting more near misses is that it is a hassle to report. In our consulting work we have noticed that near-miss reporting systems can tend to get overly complicated in an effort to be thorough. Work to resist that temptation.

Positively Reinforce Reporting

The science has taught us that what gets reinforced gets done, so be creative in figuring out ways to strengthen the behavior of reporting a near miss through positive reinforcement. Initially it is important to acknowledge and celebrate the reporting of near misses. For example, one client had senior leaders send a thank you email when a quality near miss was reported. Another client used casino-grade poker chips as a tangible signal of appreciation for reporting a near miss.[1]

In addition to timely acknowledgement of reporting, keep in mind that for many employees, making a difference is a positive reinforcer. Noticing or experiencing valuable outputs from the near-miss reporting system can function to increase the behavior of reporting. Many employees describe typical near-miss reporting systems as a "black box" where they submit reports and then nothing seems to happen. While

The sense that one has made a difference is a reinforcer for many.

---

[1] See Appendix H: *Near-Miss Reporting: Best Practices from Brown-Forman.*

someone may well be analyzing the data and making decisions and even improvements with their inputs, that may not be obvious to the person reporting. Make it obvious: identify or create targeted outputs that highlight improvements made based on near misses entered into the system.

For example, some clients provide visible feedback on the steps taken and/or changes made in a facility due to near-miss reporting. One organization used to dedicate a safety meeting every other week to show pictures of all the recent changes and improvements that had been made as a result of near misses reported and safety work orders submitted. This became powerful visual feedback that showed those reporting they were making a difference. Many employees related that it effectively served as positive reinforcement for their submitting of near misses into the system.

In addition to this type of general feedback, some of our clients have had great success providing more streamlined, organized insights that are useful to someone performing a certain type of task. For example, provide a brief summary of key learnings gleaned from recent near misses related to confined space entry to work teams preparing to perform a task in confined space. Such targeted insights are far more useful feedback than a company-wide email every time a near miss is reported into the system, and far less likely to fade into the background noise.

Eliminate Punishment for Reporting

As noted in Chapter 3, punishment is anything that follows a behavior and makes it less likely to occur. The effect of punishment is not linked to intention. It is possible to punish the very behavior we want, and that is often the case in near-miss reporting systems. As such, it is important to be vigilant in identifying and eliminating any punishment for the behavior of reporting near misses. More often than not, this punishment is inadvertent. Even well-intended systems can discourage people from reporting by being overly time-consuming and creating fear and/or embarrassment. Behavioral science provides the lens to assess systems for these inadvertent consequences. Then leaders can adjust the systems to ensure the prerequisite behavior (reporting) gets reinforced.

As in the scenario at the start of the chapter, an employee who reports a near miss and experiences a barrage of phone calls and email inquiries from

It is possible to punish the very behavior we want, and that is often the case in near-miss reporting systems.

many levels of management may question the value of reporting the next time. Similarly, if a near miss sheds an unfavorable light on an area of your business as a result of being shared far and wide, that can inhibit reporting. Some clients have established a single point of contact to follow up with the reporting party and minimize the barrage of calls. Others have enabled anonymous reporting systems to glean the key elements from a near miss without it reflecting poorly on an individual or work group.

Evaluate Intention vs Impact

An important senior leader behavior is verifying the effectiveness of systems and processes. Rather than acting simply as another level of audit while out in the operation, senior leaders should adopt a big-picture, systems view and seek input on how organizational processes and systems are functioning day-to-day. Checking up on near-miss reporting systems is a perfect example. Much like in the television show "Undercover Boss," senior leaders are often shocked by what they learn about systems they have created.

At times the unintended ripple effect of a system, decision, or policy change can have drastic consequences at the front lines of the organization. If senior leaders demonstrate that their intent is to learn and improve, they find that people across the organization are willing to share their concerns and experiences. Leaders need only ask the right questions, and then ensure anything that follows functions as positive reinforcement for employees providing candid upward feedback.

Near-miss reporting systems are designed to encourage reporting in order to facilitate organizational learning and prevention. Thus, they should be evaluated against those aims—does an increase in reporting lead to safety improvement? Resist getting caught up in quotas or worrying about getting too many poor-quality near-miss reports. Sound behavioral advice when attempting to improve any kind of behavior is to reinforce quantity first, then reinforce quality. The more near misses that get reported, the more quality reports there will be and the more opportunities there will be to learn and improve. Several clients have used behavioral strategies to increase near-miss reporting and have impressive data showing an associated decrease in incidents.[2] These kinds of data are demonstrating that the near-miss system is functioning as intended.

Keeping these five tips in mind will enable you to better align your impact with your intentions and yield the organizational learning and prevention that your near-miss reporting system was designed to enable.

---

[2] See Appendix I: *Clark Pacific's Safety Journey.*

CHAPTER 10

INCIDENT INVESTIGATIONS

One of our clients in the natural gas infrastructure business had a division where almost all work was performed by contractors or service partners. While they had a robust incident investigation process, they struggled to get investigations done completely within the KPI timeframe of 21 days. Candid participation by the involved parties was difficult at best. Contract employees were reluctant to open up about incidents for fear they would lose the contract. There was frustration at all levels around the process and it was clear that investigations were not painting a clear picture of what happened, and more importantly, how to ensure the incident didn't happen again.

Changing the Blame Game

Incident Investigations are a cornerstone of any safety management system. When investigations are done well, incidents provide opportunities to learn and improve. Unfortunately, it can be very difficult to do good investigations because of reluctance on the part of employees to be completely candid. Fear of negative repercussions dampens willingness to be honest. While the intention of most incident investigations is not to assign blame or apply negative consequences, the emphasis certainly tends to drift there over time, and the perception in the field is often that finding someone

75

to blame and punish is the inevitable outcome. In the natural gas example, the knowledge that jobs were on the line led to incomplete and protracted incident investigations. Management was upset that the 21-day turnaround time was often missed, which led to pressure to close investigations before fully complete. Investigations rarely got to true root causes and therefore had limited credibility with those doing the work.

When investigations are focused carefully and deliberately on learning and prevention—not finding fault, then full candor and enhanced learning and prevention is far more likely. This is exactly what the natural gas infrastructure company did.

When investigations are focused on learning and prevention—not finding fault, then candor is far more likely.

As part of a broader organizational effort to improve safety culture, the company communicated an emphasis on "Reporting, Trust and Learning." With that focus, they made changes to their incident investigations that they summarized to their contractors this way, "We are not interested in fault or blame; we only want to know what really happened so we can prevent it from happening again." Assurances were given that contractors would not lose their contract for having an incident, but they certainly would for not being forthcoming during investigations.

This change in focus, the assurances provided, and the credibility they'd earned by doing what they said they would do produced radically different results that were replicated in a short period of time. With a singular shared purpose of learning to enable prevention, company personnel and contractors alike were quick to share what they knew. Root causes were being identified in a fraction of the time, instead of missing deadlines as they had. More relevant information allowed better analyses of the situation. And the findings were seen as more credible in the field because they weren't singling out the individual performer but looking at how the performer operated within the system. They identified what could be done differently to set everyone up to succeed and work safely. Management kept its word and did not punish service partners for having an incident. They did, however, part ways with one contractor found to have concealed information during an investigation. In this way, they matched their words with their actions and created a stepwise change in the efficiency and the effectiveness of their investigations.

By focusing on building trust, encouraging honest reporting, and having learning and improvement as the goal, organizations can dramatically improve the investigation process. The adage "quality in, quality out" absolutely applies to the investigation process. A big part of the "quality in" comes down to what employees report during investigations. Someone who is fearful of blame and discipline will not share openly and honestly. So how do you move from fear of reporting to candid reporting? From a behavioral science perspective, candid reporting is a discretionary behavior. Employees do not have to be completely candid when there are no witnesses or witnesses are willing to be complicit. Thus, honest reporting is discretionary. We know from the science that discretionary behaviors only happen in the context of positive reinforcement. Admitting mistakes, bubbling up bad news early, and describing accurately what a coworker has done—such behaviors will only take place if those reporting see the value or benefit (positive consequences) and if they are confident there will be no undesired repercussions (negative consequences). So, transitioning from a culture in which there is fear of being candid in investigations to one in which candor is the norm, requires a lot of positive reinforcement in and around the investigation process and for candid reporting in particular.

The Power of Trust

As we have already established, trust is necessary for reporting, and reporting is essential for learning. Trust then is paramount for prevention. That said, it is wise to assume that many employees' experience and expectations are that telling the truth in investigations will lead to negative consequences. Thus, leaders must work to build trust. The litmus test for each leader should be, "Will this action/decision build trust or erode trust?" If you are successful in establishing that your primary interest in investigations is continuous improvement, learning, and prevention, then your analyses will be more comprehensive and your findings more useful to the field. This will function as positive reinforcement for future candid participation in investigations.

Trust is paramount for prevention.

Returning to the gas infrastructure business, a later investigation showed the progress made as a result of the focus on building trust and reinforcing candor and learning. The incident involved a crew responding to an inquiry about an issue with a buried pipe. The safest means to explore the condition was open trench excavation. But the property owner and local municipality had an important event on the weekend, so a decision was made to use remote sensing to explore the situation more quickly than by open trench. The drills used to probe and conduct remote sensing encountered an obstruction underground that was not reflected in the maps and diagrams of the subsurface. Unfortunately, an employee operating a drill caused a vibration that in turn created a small leak in the pipe, which then necessitated open trench excavation to repair.

When the investigation was performed on the incident, it was quickly determined that the frontline crew did everything they were instructed to do and were supposed to do. They referenced the maps throughout the job. They conducted all their pre-job briefs and post-job debriefs. They followed all applicable procedures. Even though the drill operator created the leak, the root cause was determined to be back at headquarters: the scheduling department who agreed to do the work using the less safe means, just to meet the artificial deadline created by the municipality and property owner. The original job itself was non-critical and could have just as easily been scheduled for the following week when there was sufficient time for the safer open trench excavation approach.

The above investigation was completed in four days instead of the typical 21. All parties actively engaged in sharing what happened and how they viewed it from their vantage point. Because the objective was to learn and prevent (and not to discipline), there was limited debate over what the underlying causes were. And because the solution in this example rested in scheduling, they learned about the unintended ripple effect of their decisions. A new best practice was created where scheduling would communicate and calibrate with the crew in the field before making schedule commitments to the customer.

Beyond Behavior as a Root Cause

Another common shortcoming of typical incident investigations is that when behavior is identified as a root cause, many investigations go no further. Unfortunately, stopping at "individual's decision," "operator error," "employee distraction," or "complacency" rarely gets to an actionable response that effectively decreases recurrence. These statements beg the question, "Why?" Why did the operator, who has been trained and knows how to do the task correctly, make an error? Why was the worker distracted? Why did they violate a rule? As noted, the science of

Operator error is not a root cause.

behavior provides a methodology for answering these questions. Taking the time to understand why performers acted as they did often reveals system or process factors that contributed to the at-risk behavior. It is important to remember that an individual's behavior makes perfect sense to him or her in that moment. Only when we view the situation from the performer's perspective at the time they took the action in question, are we able to better see all the antecedents and consequences that led to that behavior.

Conducting More Impactful Incident Investigations

To ensure that your efforts are aligned with the intention of learning and prevention, and to enable a deep dive into any behavioral root causes, there are several practical steps you can follow to optimize incident investigations:

1. Understand the current-state perception of your incident investigation process and make adjustments to ensure candid, robust participation in the discovery phase. If you can redirect from fault/blame to learning/understanding, you are more likely to hear what truly happened.

2. Acknowledge any past practices that may have served to erode trust, either in the process or in management. Admitting missteps or recognizing where past actions may have produced unintended downstream effects will help to build trust.

3. Make specific commitments for how you will conduct incident investigations going forward. Only make promises that you know you can keep. If you can assure that discipline will only be invoked if specific criteria are met (e.g., willful violation of procedures, falsification, working under the influence), then you will yield more candor.

4. When your analyses point to individual behavior as a cause, explore it in context. Analyze behaviors and practices prior

to the event, not just those directly related to the incident. If frontline at-risk behaviors have occurred before there was an incident but very little was said or done about them, then you must explore the leadership practices as well. In that case, there is more than one performer who contributed to the incident and addressing only the frontline performer will suboptimize your analysis and erode credibility. Critically probe how systems and processes may have influenced behavior. See the DE³ Checklist® in Chapter 4 for a list of systems to consider.

5. Involve those closest to the work in the analyses and proposed solutions.

While these additional steps (building trust to ensure candor and doing a deeper dive to understand behavioral root causes) will take more time, the information gleaned from incident investigations is so valuable, it is worth the time and effort to improve the process.

CHAPTER 11

HAZARD IDENTIFICATION AND REMEDIATION

A few years ago, we consulted with a safety professional who took a new job as a corporate safety manager at another large, multi-site company. After touring all her sites to get a feel for the state of safety, she called us very concerned. During her tours she saw uncontrolled hazards at most sites that in her previous company would have been dealt with immediately. She reported that when she asked frontline workers and managers about the hazards, she got a lot of "deer in the headlights" looks. In addition to some process and training issues, she knew there were behavioral issues but wasn't sure what all the behaviors were or where to begin. Did workers just not see the hazards? Did they see them but not report them? Did they report them but they never got addressed? Was hazard remediation not a priority for management? We worked with her and the sites to identify the behavioral contributors to the problem, and solutions to address them. Not surprisingly, this company was not unique in its struggles around hazard identification and remediation.

Identifying and controlling hazards in order to mitigate risk is a critical component of a good safety management system. There are a variety of systems and processes that organizations use to achieve this goal including site-wide risk assessments done by safety professionals, pre-task risk assessments done by frontline workers prior to tasks, work order systems that prioritize repairs that have a safety component, hazard identification training, and hazard remediation processes. There are behavioral components in all these systems and if those components are not working well, the science of behavior can help. As noted previously, there are some common categories of behaviors that many organizations struggle with.

Truly effective risk management requires active participation by frontline employees.

While hazard identification and remediation typically involves several groups and individuals (e.g., safety professionals, risk management professionals, Management of Change teams) in this chapter we focus on operations employees. Truly effective risk management requires active participation by leaders and their frontline employees whose work exposes them to the hazards. Active participation by this group is sometimes difficult to get and/ or sustain. Below are the behavior categories that are frequently a challenge for many organizations.

1. Looking for and identifying hazards.

2. Reporting hazards through appropriate channels.

3. Addressing (controlling) hazards.

4. Following up to communicate remediation and ensure the controls are sustainable.

Improving the consistency of these behaviors will contribute to the broader risk mitigation efforts and thus improve safety.

Looking for Hazards

The ability to identify hazards is a prerequisite to engage employees in risk management. Since many hazards are not obvious, it is essential to train employees at all levels in the potential hazards in the industry, department, and particular work being done. Classroom training is a good starting point but is usually not sufficient. Some form of on-the-job training and/or modeling is helpful. An Oklahoma oil and gas exploration operation we worked with developed an informal but effective process for doing just that. During every crew changeover meeting, all contractors met in the "safety shack" prior to starting their 12-hour shift to discuss what they'd done the previous day to make the operation safer. They prompted workers to share hazards they had identified (no matter how small) and what they did about them. The sharing of identified hazards helped all workers, especially the newer people know what to look for and motivated them to look. As one of the newer, "greenhorn" roustabouts on the job said, "It makes me look harder every day to find and report hazards."

While training in hazard identification is essential, even trained people are unlikely to persist in looking for hazards unless there is reinforcement for doing so. As with any other behavior, scanning for hazards is a function of its consequences. If there are no consequences that maintain the behavior, it will fade. Thus, good hazard processes must include strategies to positively reinforce the behavior of looking for hazards. In the example above, the reinforcement was built into the daily meetings. Every hazard reported was acknowledged, discussed, and dealt with, which is the perfect reinforcement for the behavior of looking.[1]

Like all behavior, scanning for hazards is a function of its consequences.

Most companies have formal processes to encourage workers to look for hazards prior to doing work. Pre-task Risk Assessments, SLAMs (stop, look, assess, manage), Job Hazard Analyses, etc. use checklists to prompt looking for hazards, discussing how to control for the hazards, and stopping work if control is not possible.

---

[1] See Appendix J: *Making Safety Hazard Scans Realtime Habits,* for tips on facilitating frequent hazard scans.

Unfortunately, such tools are easily pencil whipped and thus rendered ineffective. Leaders must go beyond just holding workers accountable for completing the checklist and reinforce the quality of the assessments. For example, a large mining company we worked with knew that consistent, quality execution of their pre-task risk assessment tool would prevent injuries. We helped them design a coaching process in which supervisors asked questions of frontline workers at some point during a job for which they had done a pre-task risk assessment. Rather than just asking if the risk assessment was done, supervisors asked how the workers implemented controls based on the assessment. The goal was to link doing a good job on the assessment to meaningful changes that helped keep them safe. Workers not only did the assessments more consistently, but they also saw true value in doing them well, and no longer considered them just another piece of paperwork to be done. It was also an opportunity for supervisors to coach employees on using Stop Work Authority if hazards could not be controlled.[2]

Reporting Hazards

Once you are sure that employees know how to recognize hazards and they are consistently scanning for hazards, the next step is either to control the hazard if possible (more on this in the next section) or report the hazard for others to address. Unfortunately, many organizations inadvertently discourage reporting. A perfect example comes from a client at the very start of our work with them. We were getting a tour of the facility and observed a tank that was leaking fluid out into the walkway. Our hosts didn't appear to notice the fluid. During a focus group later that day we asked a few of the operators about the hazard. "We've learned to just work around that," was the response. After probing further,

---

[2] Hazard remediation also includes assessing the level of risk particular hazards pose, but that is beyond the scope of this book.

the hourly personnel said that they had reported the hazard on several prior occasions, but nothing ever seemed to come from it. Over time, they accepted the situation as the norm and just learned to walk around the slick area.

This scenario is all too typical—employees report a hazard and nothing appears to be done about it. Sometimes this is a function of a poor reporting system (e.g., the employee tells a supervisor in passing, and the supervisor gets busy and forgets to deal with it), and sometimes it is a function of budget—waiting on parts for repair, capital request delays, or higher priority hazards that need to be dealt with. Regardless of the reason, if there is no communication back to employees, the behavior of reporting is in jeopardy.

The science shows us that behaviors that do not get reinforced undergo what is called extinction. The scenario above is a classic example. Over time, if reporting does not result in hazards being controlled, people stop reporting. Of course, it is impossible to control every hazard immediately. Workers understand that it may take time, so an interim reinforcer can be leaders immediately acknowledging the report, providing a temporary solution to ensure safety, and providing timely updates on progress toward a permanent solution. Ultimately the best reinforcer is the natural reinforcer—the

Over time, if reporting does not result in hazards being controlled, workers stop reporting.

hazard gets eliminated or controlled. Evidence of movement toward that goal will also reinforce the behavior of reporting.

Addressing Hazards

When possible, workers should address hazards as they identify them. We have talked to many a frustrated leader and safety professional who complain that workers report hazards that they themselves could control. There are many reasons workers may resist taking care of hazards themselves including being uncertain if their control is appropriate, fear of negative repercussions if not, wanting to avoid being accountable, and not having enough time. Encouraging workers to address hazards themselves requires positive reinforcement, just like any other behavior. Remember that "keeping yourself safe" is a future uncertain consequence that can't compete with the more immediate and certain consequences associated with passing it along to others. A great example of effective reinforcement was created by a young safety professional who would take pictures of hazards that had been controlled by frontline workers and share them at tailgate meetings. If he ran across an attempt at controlling a hazard that failed, he was sure to reinforce the attempt and involve the employee in troubleshooting a different solution.

The most important reinforcer for the behaviors of looking for and reporting hazards is addressing the hazards in a timely way.

There are clearly some hazards that appropriately get escalated to management, maintenance, risk management teams or other individuals or groups. When this happens, it is essential that receipt of the hazard report is acknowledged immediately. Remember, immediate and certain consequences are the most powerful. Some acknowledgement of and appreciation for the act of reporting will prevent the perception that reported hazards go into the black hole and ultimately avoid extinction.

As we have said, the most important reinforcer for the behaviors of looking for and reporting hazards is **addressing hazards in a timely way**. When quick fixes are impossible (because they require capital investments, waiting on parts, etc.) then an interim fix should be established and clear and frequent feedback on the status of the more permanent fix will serve as an effective reinforcer.[3]

Follow-Up

While the most important follow-up is controlling the hazard or communicating the status toward control, there are some additional types of follow-up that are important to strengthen the behaviors of scanning for and reporting hazards.

Sometimes it is difficult to notice when a hazard has been controlled. Just as we often don't notice when a minor ache or pain is gone, we often don't notice the absence of a hazard. This is why communicating that the hazard was eliminated or controlled (and how) is important for reinforcing the behaviors of looking for and reporting hazards.

A second type of follow-up that is important is checking to see if the controls worked. If the hazard wasn't eliminated, did the controls put in place work to reduce or eliminate the risk? This is especially important if the controls were on the lower end of the Hierarchy of Controls. Some engineering controls (e.g., machine guards), all administrative controls, and all PPE controls, are only effective if the associated worker behaviors occur consistently. Follow-up is required to ensure the controls are effective and to add controls if necessary.

In summary, controlling hazards and reducing risk is complex work involving behaviors at all levels of the organization. If your systems aren't working as planned, assess what might be discouraging the critical behaviors (looking, reporting, fixing, following

---

[3] The Hierarchy of Controls should always guide decisions on how to address hazards, with elimination of the hazard as the ideal choice. Behavioral workarounds are typically the weakest level of control but are sometimes necessary.

up) and make changes to the organizational systems (including management systems) to better support those behaviors. Including hazard remediation as a leading indicator and holding management accountable for the behaviors to make the system work is an ideal way to ensure this critical part of your safety management system is optimally effective.

CHAPTER 12

LIFESAVING RULES FOR SIF PREVENTION

Like other high-performing organizations in the mining industry, this client had a heavy focus on fatality prevention. They identified the tasks that presented the highest risk for serious injuries and fatalities and created a process to manage the risk. The process was exemplary— clear expectations, good training, identification of lifesaving rules and a process for checking on adherence to those rules, including tracking action items resulting from those checks. They focused not just on behavior, but on the conditions and systems that made following the rules more or less difficult. The process was beyond reproach. Unfortunately, they continued to have incidents and near misses around a few of the high-risk tasks. Lockout/Tagout and mobile equipment issues continued to recur. A behavior analysis revealed that while the system was well designed, some of the behavioral components were being completed haphazardly.

Serious Incident and Fatality (SIF) prevention entails many components including attention to equipment reliability, use of technology to prevent incidents, process safety, and of course, behavior. The latter tends to be the most challenging for most organizations. The typical approach is to establish clear procedures and a corresponding set of rules around the most important behaviors for preventing SIF incidents. Those rules are known by various names such as Lifesaving Rules, Golden Rules, or Cardinal Rules. The less common term "Blood Rules" graphically indicates the genesis of these rules—they come from analysis of serious injuries and fatalities within organizations and/or industries. Not surprisingly, many lifesaving rules are similar across high-hazard industries. Energy isolation, fall arrest, and safe operation of mobile equipment all show up on most lists. Lifesaving rules are helpful in that they pinpoint critical safety activities that help prevent serious injuries, fatalities, and other catastrophic events. However, an overly simplistic approach to implementing these rules undermines their potential effectiveness.

Typical Strategies

A common strategy to encourage rule-following includes the following steps:

1. Clearly state the rules in written documents, signage, and verbal communications.

2. Ensure all employees are trained in the rules and understand their importance.

3. Clearly state the consequences for not following the rules— often termination.

4. Instruct management to do checks on adherence to rules and follow through with the consequences if rules are not followed.

While these steps are important, they are not sufficient to create a culture of lifesaving habits. This approach implies that the rules are always easy to follow (which they are not) and assumes that threatening with dismissal is the best strategy to ensure adherence (which it is not).

Verification of Rule-Following

Some industry leaders go beyond frontline-focused lifesaving rules and create a set of verification protocols or controls that outline what needs to happen to enable the rules to be followed. These controls often require both management and frontline involvement. For example, using fall protection when working at height is a common lifesaving rule. The controls or protocols associated with this rule might include doing pre-task hazard assessments to determine the need for fall protection, ensuring appropriate gear is readily available, identifying anchor points prior to the task, and ensuring the gear and anchor points are inspected regularly. This dual approach of identifying lifesaving behaviors at the front line and lifesaving controls or protocols that include management behavior, is a more thorough approach to what are often complex situations. On the surface, it seems that stating the rule, "All employees must wear fall protection when working above two meters," is straightforward and should be easy to comply with, but it often is not. Differing types of fall protection, availability of fall protection, uncertainty as to when it should be used, and lack of appropriate anchor points are just some of the ways this seemingly simple rule can be hard to follow. Pinpointing behaviors on the part of leaders, aimed at ensuring systems and processes support the rules, helps set up the frontline for success, and ensures appropriate shared ownership.

Rule Enforcement: The Typical Approach

The addition of protocols or controls to lifesaving rules is helpful. However, the strategy to ensure adherence to the rules and protocols is often less effective than it could be. As noted, the most common strategy is to clarify the rules and protocols, make it clear that those caught not adhering to the rules will be terminated, and then check for compliance. In scientific terms, this involves the use of antecedents (communicating and training in the rules), negative reinforcement (telling workers to follow the rule or else be terminated), and punishment (those caught violating the rule are terminated). As we have noted, this strategy has well-documented side effects, particularly when the negative consequences are severe, as they are in the case of lifesaving rules. The most notable side effects are fear, underreporting, erosion of trust, and an "us-against-them" sentiment. Fear of being fired often leads to workers focusing more on not being caught than on problem-solving ways to better follow the rules. This would be less problematic if the rules were always easy to follow, however workplaces are often surprisingly complex and getting more complex all the time.

In order to ensure the rules are followed, you must create a culture where workers are willing to tell you when it has been difficult to follow rules.

Some workplaces, such as mines and construction sites, are constantly changing. Despite the appeal of a simple rule to "wear fall protection when working above two meters," it is often not that simple. Ultimately, in order to ensure the rule is followed, you must create a culture where workers are willing to tell you when it has been difficult to follow the rule, and tell you when they actually did not follow the rule and why (even more risky). Workers need to be willing to say that they don't know, they are unsure, or they are confused. Only through these conversations can sustainable rule adherence be achieved. To assume that it is always easy or even possible to follow lifesaving rules is to not understand the complex, fluid nature of most high-hazard work. To assume that threatening to terminate people for not following rules will ensure everyone follows them is naïve. Such an approach may make senior leaders feel good about taking decisive action, but it rarely leads to the desired outcome.

A More Effective Strategy

A better strategy for implementing lifesaving rules and verification protocols is a little more complex, but necessary, and involves the addition of these interrelated steps:

- **Positively Reinforce Stop Work Authority.** Empowering workers to stop work if they believe they cannot do the job safely is an important component of any safety management system, but it is particularly important in the context of lifesaving rules. When following lifesaving rules or protocols is difficult or confusing, employees at all levels must be comfortable stopping work and resolving the issue. Many organizations understand this and thus promote Stop Work Authority. However, just giving workers permission to stop work is not enough. Stop Work needs to be positively reinforced, both actively and aggressively, because the natural consequences discourage it. Workers understand the importance of production (and sometimes are working under production incentives) so while they may not fear getting in trouble for stopping work, they are reluctant to do so because they anticipate the negative impact on production. However, Stop Work provides an excellent opportunity to evaluate the situations where the rules and protocols might not be easily followed. Equally important, there may be circumstances where the hazard controls and rules do not adequately mitigate the hazards. This is especially true in work settings that are constantly changing. New hazards may have emerged that require adjustments to the rules. Thus, the more workers stop work and engage with leaders to do some

Stop Work Authority must be positively reinforced because the natural consequences discourage it.

problem solving, the more robust the rules and protocols will be, and the more likely they will be followed.

- **Build trust.** As noted in Chapter 5, trust plays a central role in safety. Dealing with the complexity that can surround life-saving rules and protocols requires an open and honest learning culture focused on joint problem solving between management and the front line. Proactively working on building trust is an essential prerequisite to creating lifesaving habits. To reiterate, some key leadership behaviors that build trust include asking more than telling, actively listening, doing what you say you will do, acknowledging management's role in problems, and using more positive than negative consequences (see Chapter 5 for a more thorough discussion of how to build trust).

- **Perform frequent observations.** Leaders should plan to do many observations of tasks involving lifesaving rules. These observations should be less about checking on rule adherence, and more about conversations that help both parties identify and understand how and when the rules are hard to follow and then identify ways to make them easier. If workers believe the observations are in place to catch them doing something wrong, they will be guarded, and the conversations will be less productive. Leaders need to make it safe and comfortable for workers to talk about why and how the rules may be hard to follow. A focus on the physical conditions and organizational systems will make clear that the goal is not to correct behavior, but to better enable adhering to lifesaving rules.

- **Positively reinforce rule-following.** Most organizations plan to use consequences only when rules are not followed. But the science is clear—positively reinforcing adherence to the rules/protocols is the only way to ensure consistent rule-following. Furthermore, when people experience more positive reinforcement for doing things right, they are more likely to believe that the rules are truly about keeping them safe as opposed to regulatory compliance for the company or checking a box for management. There is one caveat. It is important to avoid reinforcing following a rule at all costs. As noted previously, there may be circumstances in which emerging hazards require stopping work and reassessing, rather than blindly following the rule. Stopping work and reassessing the hazards and controls should always be the overarching behavior if there is any uncertainty.

- **Positive accountability for verification protocols.** While the focus tends to be on the lifesaving rules at the front line, an equally important set of behaviors is ensuring leaders engage in the protocols or controls designed to ensure rules are followed. As discussed, the quality of the interactions leaders have with the front line is paramount. Leaders need to set the context for productive conversations about enabling rule-following and positively reinforce rule-following when they see it. Getting these leadership activities to happen regularly requires education and accountability to ensure busy leaders make the time. Without accountability leaders will too often default to tasks that do have tight accountabilities. Progressive companies understand this and are working to educate and coach their leaders in more positive strategies for managing lifesaving rules, including building in accountability to do so.

Clearly, these steps are more complicated and time-consuming than just stating a rule and punishing those who don't follow it, but lifesaving rules and protocols are rarely simple. Proceeding as though they are will ultimately undermine the goal of preventing fatalities. There are no more important behaviors to manage than those associated with lifesaving rules. Investing in managing them effectively is the most important protocol of all.

CHAPTER 13

SETTING A GOAL
OF ZERO

The VP of Operations came back from the conference pumped. He was determined to improve safety and heard several great talks that gave him some good ideas on how to proceed. One idea in particular caught his attention. The idea was that the only acceptable goal in safety is zero incidents. As he listened to the presenter make the case, he became more and more convinced. He came back to the plant excited to start a Goal of Zero campaign. He was convinced that setting a goal of zero incidents would be inspirational and motivational. He was surprised when he presented his idea to the safety staff, and they expressed concern.

In an attempt to improve safety performance, many organizations publicly set a "zero injuries" goal. For some, it is a stretch goal, for others it is within reach, and for a few it has been achieved (but often not sustained). From an ethical perspective, companies must strive for zero harm. In actuality, it is always the unspoken goal that all employees go home safely every day. However, is there value in setting a numeric goal of zero and implementing a public campaign around it? Some leaders view it as a bold demonstration of the importance of safety. But as with any goal, how you go about communicating the goal, and more importantly, managing toward that end goal, matters a great deal. The same goal can in fact lead to the development of very different safety cultures and practices, and very different outcomes.

Incidents as Preventable

One thing setting a goal of zero can do is signal that management believes that all incidents are preventable and therefore intends to work relentlessly on prevention. In this case, leading indicators become the focus of management efforts—not the goal of zero. When management emphasizes preventative activities such as eliminating hazards, reporting all near misses, conducting quality pre-task risk assessments, improving the safety of work processes, and investing in improved safety leadership, a proactive and preventative culture develops. Achieving this kind of culture also requires minimizing negative consequences associated with reporting of incidents—even when the reporting of a recordable incident, by definition, means the goal of zero will not be achieved. As we have noted, driving fear out of safety requires treating all errors, problems, near misses and incidents as opportunities to learn and using forward-looking accountability to ensure learnings are implemented and lead to improvement. It also requires sophisticated and strategic use of positive reinforcement—reinforcing preventative behaviors, not lack of accidents. This approach to managing safety is the only way to truly achieve the goal of zero.

Incidents as Unacceptable

Alternatively, setting a goal of zero can communicate that incidents will not be tolerated. This occurs when leaders persist in using lagging indicators to measure and manage safety. If leaders state the goal is zero and indicate that anything other than zero is unacceptable, they may believe they are "being tough on safety," but unfortunately it sets the stage for many undesirable activities and behaviors. Developing "creative" strategies for determining what counts as a recordable incident and instituting discipline for incidents are just two examples of undesired practices that can develop as people do whatever it takes to meet the goal.

The most damaging outcome of communicating that incidents are unacceptable is underreporting. As discussed in Chapter 8, leaders never want to believe underreporting is occurring, but it is an inevitable outcome of managing safety with fear. As discussed, negative reinforcement and punishment (the consequences that create fear) are default management tools and thus the default strategy when a goal of zero is set. In other words, if leaders don't specify, measure and manage the preventative activities that will lead to zero, then people will do whatever it takes to get to zero. In the case of safety, the easiest thing to do is not report incidents. The science of behavior predicts this and it has proven true in organization after organization.

Fear-based cultures are not the only possible negative outcome of a goal of zero. Some organizations attempt to get to zero using what they erroneously believe to be positive reinforcement—setting up incentive systems and contests that reward employees for not having incidents. However, as discussed in Chapter 8, if the only measure is the number of incidents, the outcome is often the same. People will not report.

The Paradox of a Goal of Zero

While setting a goal of zero is always done with the best of intentions, if positive and proactive management of preventative activities is not used, it too often leads to undesirable activities that ultimately prevent getting to zero. The only way to achieve zero is to know what is really going on in the workplace so that hazards and error-likely situations can be identified and improved. That requires reporting all incidents and near misses, which in turn requires positively reinforcing reporting, by letting people know reporting is helpful. Ironically, getting to zero requires positively reinforcing the very thing that ensures you won't achieve your goal (at least for a period of time). It is a paradox, but make no mistake, there is no other way. If the behavior of reporting is met with anything other than positive reinforcement, you will create fear of reporting. When there is fear of reporting, fear of failing, or fear of acknowledging that things are not perfectly safe, the goal of zero is out of reach and in some cases, the goal can be a recipe for disaster, as important precursors of potential catastrophes are hidden.

Ironically, getting to zero requires positively reinforcing the very thing that ensures you won't achieve your goal (at least for a period of time).

Given all this complexity, the goal of zero incidents is controversial. Some debate whether zero is even possible while others think setting a goal of zero is essential. Many see the undesired effects described above and think it is a bad idea. One thing is certain, just stating a goal of zero is not helpful. Goals alone don't improve anything. How safety is managed is what ultimately matters. When organizations manage with leading indicators—when they manage what people do to prevent incidents—they are on the path to zero. Regardless of lagging indicator goals, leaders must create a safety culture that encourages all employees to behave as if zero is the goal and set about doing the things required to achieve it.

CHAPTER 14

SAFETY
TECHNOLOGY

The safety group was excited. They were finally going to be able to permanently address speeding in company vehicles. The newly installed GPS devices enabled the tracking of vehicle location, direction, braking and most importantly, speed. They marveled at the power of technology to address otherwise stubborn at-risk behaviors such as speeding. Once the devices were installed management received email alerts when there were speeding events. Managers then spoke to drivers about the speeding events at the end of their shift. The ability to know about all speeding events and provide more frequent consequences for speeding seemed like the ideal solution to the problem. Within a few weeks there were reports of some of the devices not working properly. Investigations revealed the devices had been tampered with in a variety of ways, all with the goal of disabling them.

Technology has truly transformed the workplace and the impact on safety is only beginning to be felt. Robots that can do the most dangerous jobs, monitoring devices that set off alarms to wake drivers when they nod off, devices that can stop vehicles if collisions are imminent, and smart PPE that can monitor heart rate and temperature are a few examples. Technology has the potential to dramatically reduce illness and injury, but it also creates some behavioral challenges. We are going to address two categories of safety technology with behavioral implications: performance monitoring and automation.

Performance Monitoring

Technology enables the monitoring of many aspects of performance that previously was only accessible through human observation. No longer do managers and supervisors have to go out in the field to observe work; sensors and cameras collect data and send performance summaries to their computers. While managers greatly appreciate such technology, not surprisingly, those whose behavior is being monitored often resist it. To them it can feel like Big Brother.[1] Behavioral science can help organizations avoid resistance, improve adoption, and maximize utilization of performance monitoring technology. After all, it is not the technology itself that people resist (as evidenced by the fact that very few people resist using cell phones). It is how management uses technology to manage behavior that matters. Pairing technology with positive consequences can facilitate adoption. Pairing technology with negative consequences can lead to anger, resentment, and sabotage (as was the case in the scenario at the beginning of the chapter).

It is not technology itself that people resist, it is how management uses technology to manage behavior that matters.

Whether technology is preventing at-risk behavior (e.g., sensors that stop vehicles if a collision is imminent) or simply monitoring behavior (GPS that tracks speed and braking events), technological devices are always collecting data. The sheer volume of data

---

[1] Privacy and ethical issues associated with the use of technology in the workplace are beyond the scope of this book and our recommendations assume such issues have been addressed prior to an organization adopting technology.

collected can influence decisions around how to use it. For example, assuming most workers drive the speed limit the vast majority of the time, it seems most efficient to only send alerts to management when there are significant speeding events. However, sending alerts only when at-risk behavior occurs leads to the overuse of negative consequences. The technology simply becomes a bigger stick to beat people with.

The true potential of having data on so much behavior is not that you can see every instance of at-risk behavior, but rather that you can see every instance of safe behavior. More importantly, you can see improvement in safe behavior. As noted in Chapter 3, research shows that the best way to increase desired behavior is by positively reinforcing improvement over time. Technology enables management to see small improvements, which enables the use of more immediate and certain positive consequences, which accelerates behavior change. Furthermore, technology helps leaders achieve the optimal balance of positive to negative consequences (4:1).[2]

The true potential of having data on so much behavior is not that you can see every instance of at-risk behavior, but rather that you can see every instance of safe behavior.

But the potential doesn't end there. Technology enables gamification of safety improvement. Challenges to beat your own best performance, or teams competing for the longest streak of safe runs are another way to build in positive consequences for safe behavior. Technology can make safety fun—imagine that. In addition, technology enables embedding positive consequences in

---

[2] The ideal ratio of positive to negative consequence use, over time, is four positives to every one negative. See https://www.aubreydaniels.com/4-to-1-Ratio for more information.

the systems themselves (e.g., green lights indicating consistent safe behavior, audio signals marking improvements or extending a streak of safe performance). Embedded consequences are some of the most powerful because they are always immediate and certain. The ability to tap into multiple sources of positive reinforcement is one of the big benefits of technology. We know from the science that the more sources of reinforcement, the faster behavior changes, and the more sustainable those changes are.

Returning to the opening scenario, if you understand behavior scientifically, it is no surprise that drivers tampered with GPS devices. Humans are wired to avoid negative consequences. Avoidance is often the mother of creative and sometimes destructive workarounds. The solution in this case is to reprogram the alerts to be sent both when significant speeding occurs and when drivers go for periods of time with no speeding events, especially for those drivers who have had speeding events in the past. This then allows positive reinforcement for improvement. But changes to alerts are just the first step. Leaders need to be trained in and held

Positive reinforcement is one of the most powerful tools in a manager's tool belt.

accountable for using positive consequences and shaping desired behavior over time. Do not assume managers will do this naturally. Most will not. It requires training and deliberate effort. But the payoff is well worth it. Positive reinforcement is one of the most powerful (and underutilized) tools in a manager's tool belt. When used well, it not only strengthens desired behaviors and builds engagement, but it increases the effectiveness of constructive feedback. Most workers are okay with feedback on at-risk behavior if improvement in that behavior is also recognized, and other desired behavior is positively reinforced.

If your organization is using (or considering using) monitoring technology to improve safe behavior, the primary question to ask is how can technology be used to strengthen safe behavior through positive reinforcement. Avoid the trap of choosing exception management and negative consequences. Careful consideration of how data will be used can avoid resistance and ensure workers welcome safety technology as they do the latest smart phone.

Automation

The second category of safety technology with behavioral implications is automation. Increasingly, robots and other types of computer-assisted technology are being used to complete critical tasks, thereby avoiding the potential for human error. While such technology has improved safety and efficiency greatly, it has downsides. With the actual work being done by computers, humans are relegated to monitoring jobs. Power plant operators who used to walk the plant checking gauges and making adjustments are now sitting in control rooms looking at an array of computer screens all day. Their job is to look for problems or deviations. Problems/deviations are rare, which is good for the organization, but bad for the behavior of monitoring. The behavior of monitoring is reinforced (maintained) by seeing something that needs responding to. As technology improves, even the problems/deviations are self-corrected by the electronic systems, so workers monitor for long periods of time and see nothing that requires a response. It should be no surprise that keeping operators awake and focused on monitoring is a big problem in many organizations. There is simply not enough reinforcement to stay engaged in the monitoring task. The scientific term for this is extinction—behavior weakens due to a lack of reinforcement. Dr. Aubrey Daniels has written and spoken about this for several years and his advice is to periodically engineer in something for workers to "catch" in order to maintain the behavior.[3]

---

[3] See Appendix F: *Combatting The Rare Error*, for more on solutions to monitoring challenges.

The second problem associated with automation is something called *deskilling*. When the work is automated, operators lose their knowledge and skills due to lack of practice. Our colleague Dr. Cloyd Hyten, an aviation buff, discussed this issue and provided a tragic example in a blog post.

There is a paradox in how technology affects safety at present. Overall, safety has been much improved by increasing automation and assisting technologies, but what happens when those technologies fail, as they inevitably will do? In fact, there is evidence that the human operators may not be prepared to handle these situations manually. In these circumstances the level of technology is making things less safe.

Take an aviation industry example. In 2009, in one of the most disturbing air crashes ever, Air France 447 fell out of the sky from 35,000 feet into the Atlantic Ocean killing all on board. The Airbus A330 had an airspeed sensor failure while flying through icy conditions, and the pilots reacted in ways that stalled the aircraft. Despite having three pilots in the cockpit trying to solve a very solvable problem, the pilots never figured out how to recover the plane before its fatal impact. Standard nose-down stall recovery maneuvers could have saved the aircraft if used after the onset of the stall. The mystery was why didn't these pilots recognize the stall and apply the proper maneuvers to recover from it? With increasing automation on fourth-generation airliners, it's not often that pilots manually fly the aircraft, and notable crashes like Air France 447 have led to much discussion of pilot deskilling. For example, the FAA published a report in 2013 on aviation automation and found that pilots were relying too much on automation to do the flying. Their very first recommendation was that pilots need more practice in manually flying the aircraft.[4]

---

[4] Hyten, Cloyd. *Is Deskilling a Threat to Safety in Your Workplace?* ADI Blog. August 25, 2015.

Pairing Behavioral Technology with Safety Technology

We have highlighted the downsides of safety technology, not to discourage its use, but to demonstrate that technological solutions alter the work environment in significant ways, and thus can alter worker behavior. Again, understanding behavior from a scientific perspective enables organizations to predict and adjust to those changes to ensure safety. If you understand that a lack of practice leads to deskilling then you can plan for practice sessions. If you understand the role of extinction in monitoring behaviors you can build in reinforcement to avoid it. If you understand the dangers of using monitoring devices to only provide corrective consequences, you can build in positive consequences to shift the balance.

Technological changes to work environments are accelerating exponentially. The need to understand the behavioral implications has never been greater.

CHAPTER 15

SUMMARY

We hope that, at a minimum, we have provided you with some helpful tips to improve safety in your organization. Ideally, we have provided you with a new lens through which to view all safety-related behaviors. Every component of your Safety Management Systems requires behavior and ensuring consistent behavior requires a scientific approach. Analyzing the systemic influences of behavior improves understanding and leads to more effective and sustainable safety solutions.

The appendices that follow are intended to provide a deeper dive into various topics covered in this book. We encourage you to go beyond this book and learn as much as you can about the science of behavior. The Suggested Readings provide many resources to continue learning. *Bringing out the Best in People* by Aubrey Daniels and *Safe by Accident: Leadership Practices that Build a Sustainable Safety Culture* by Judy Agnew and Aubrey Daniels, are great places to start.

While we encourage you to learn more, we also encourage you to simultaneously start applying what you have learned to evaluate and improve your safety systems. There are many tips throughout this book—chose one or two and try them out. Big improvements can sometimes be made with small changes.

APPENDIX ONE

IS HUMAN AND ORGANIZATIONAL PERFORMANCE (HOP) A NEW APPROACH TO SAFETY?

Judy Agnew

In the past several years, there have been articles and discussions about a "new" approach to safety called Human and Organizational Performance or HOP (it is also known as *Safety II* and *Safety Differently*). It has its foundation in the work of Sidney Dekker and James Reason and focuses on the human element of safety. It starts with the assumption that human error is inevitable and that error is a symptom of systems problems. This approach proposes (among other things) using leading versus lagging indicators; minimizing negative consequences and other strategies that drive underreporting of incidents and near misses; and including the people who do the work to identify safety solutions. I have long been a fan of Reason and Dekker. Their insistence that blame and punishment are destructive in safety is very much in keeping with the proven behavioral approach I have dedicated my professional life to. Furthermore, the belief on the part of Dekker, Reason and others that solutions to safety challenges can be found by understanding the organizational systems within which people work, also aligns with a behavioral approach.

While I agree with the tenets of HOP, what concerns me is that there have been some supporters of HOP who bill it as anti-Behavior-Based Safety (BBS). This rhetoric is either a marketing ploy by consultants trying to capitalize on anti-BBS sentiment or a fundamental misunderstanding of a behavioral approach to safety. I cannot do anything about the former, but I can address the later.

Behavior-based safety, also commonly referred to as behavioral safety, is so named because it has its foundations in the science of behavior; a scientific field of study called Behavior Analysis. Behavior Analysis seeks to understand behavior by looking at the environmental contingencies that influence behavior, past and present. Said differently, behavior is understood by looking at the context within which behavior happens; in this case the workplace. Behavior Analysis is very much a systems approach because it is understood that the influencers of behavior (antecedents and consequences) come from not just people (e.g., managers, peers), but the physical environment (e.g., equipment, layout of workspace), and organizational processes (e.g., incentives, measurement systems). In short, all organizational systems have the potential to influence safe and at-risk behavior. Once all of the variables that influence behavior are understood, adjustments can be made to make it easier for workers to work safely.

It is important to note that it is not just the frontline workers who engage in safe or at-risk behaviors. Effective BBS programs include a focus on management behavior, not just frontline behavior. Management creates and maintains the systems within which people work so their behavior (creating and maintaining systems that support safety) is an important focus of a good behavioral approach. In fact, Behavioral Safety Leadership processes have this as their primary focus. A behavioral approach (whether BBS or Safety Leadership) also helps us see the dangers of blaming frontline workers for at-risk behavior. Blaming workers for systems they don't control is unjust. Furthermore, the inevitable punishment that accompanies blame leads to workers keeping quiet about near misses, at-risk behaviors, and conditions that could lead to improved safety. As Dekker notes, blame stifles organizational learning.

Unfortunately when BBS became popular, BBS consultants and BBS processes proliferated. Some of these were clearly sub-par. In the worst cases, some programs were not based on the science of behavior at all and ended up being interpreted as "blame the worker" where a very narrow idea of behavior and its causes were proposed.

These programs were not designed by those fluent in the science of behavior and thus, failed to take the broader systems perspective. In addition they included some other fatal flaws like a focus on at-risk behavior and corrective feedback rather than a focus on strengthening safe behavior through positive strategies. Other programs, while not "blame the worker" were none-the-less designed with a superficial knowledge of behavior and thus less effective than they could have been.

Unfortunately, but understandably, these sub-par programs resulted in the rise of anti-BBS sentiment in some organizations. But to reject a behavioral approach to safety because some people miss-applied it is like rejecting antibiotics because some people don't take them correctly. Antibiotic medicines are based in science and have been proven extremely effective. However, if you don't take the correct dosage or fail to complete the full course of medicine, they won't work or won't work well. Similarly, behavioral safety is based in science and has been proven extremely effective. However, if it isn't implemented properly it won't work or won't work well.

Sustained safety improvement requires changing behavior (i.e., human performance). It requires changing the behavior of executives, managers, supervisors and frontline employees alike; behaviors related to hazard identification and remediation, behaviors related to modifying incentive systems so they don't encourage underreporting, behaviors related to developing near-miss reporting systems that truly encourage reporting, behaviors related to removing obstacles that make safe work difficult, and behaviors related to following rules and procedures. It is all behavior. Behavior is how we accomplish all of the things we need to accomplish in safety. To be anti-BBS is to ignore the proven science of behavior—the science that provides the strategies to motivate all the behaviors we need to create and sustain a safe workplace. That is akin to a drug company deciding to be anti-chemistry.

Safety practices evolve—they must in order to keep pace with changing workplaces. We must all continuously improve. There are many elements of the HOP movement that add to our understanding of and management of the human element of safety. Particularly helpful is the call for a philosophical shift to accepting human error as inevitable and looking to systems to minimize error. Also helpful is promoting the fact that setting up rule after rule, procedure after procedure and then punishing those who don't follow them only serves to decrease organizational learning. These ideas are good AND they are aligned with BBS, they are not in opposition to it. Human error is behavior. Human performance is behavior. Preventing or minimizing error requires understanding behavior. Let's not confuse people by saying that human performance is something different from human behavior. It is not.

We all have the same goal—to create safer workplaces and minimize human suffering. That requires change on the part of the humans within the organization. People are always looking for a quick fix that will solve all our complex safety problems. There are no quick fixes. What we do have is the science of behavior and it provides us with a framework to understand human performance. That framework helps us design strategies to make the necessary systems changes to support productive, safe performance. When it comes to Human and Organizational Performance (HOP) and Behavior-Based Safety (BBS), it's not an either/or. Let's keep working together, building on what we collectively have learned, and keeping the science of behavior as our foundation.

Agnew, J. & Daniels, A. (2010). *Safe by Accident? Take the Luck out of Safety.* Performance Management Publications. Atlanta, GA.

Dekker, S. (2007). *Just Culture: Balancing Safety and Accountability.* Ashgate Publishing Company. Burlington, VT.

Reason, J. (1990). *Human Error.* Press Syndicate of the University of Cambridge. New York, NY.

This article originally appeared on https://www.aubreydaniels.com/media-center/human-and-organizational-performance-hop-new-approach-safety (updated 2021).

PUNISHING PEOPLE WHO MAKE MISTAKES

Judy Agnew and Aubrey Daniels

To Punish or Not To Punish

Punishment, or *discipline* as it is usually called, is considered an important part of most safety programs, but organizations often struggle with identifying the circumstances under which it should be used. Some companies use it sparingly. Others have "zero-tolerance" policies which lead to more frequent use of punishment.

Many issues should be considered when deciding whether punishment is the right response to accidents, incidents, near misses, and at-risk behavior. Many believe that the effects of punishment are straightforward. They are not. Our purpose here is to explore punishment from a scientific perspective to enable you to make better decisions about how to respond to safety incidents. A good place to start is by answering the following important questions:

- What is the desired outcome and will punishment really lead to that outcome?
- Has punishment resulted in the desired outcome in the past?
- What side effects might punishment have, and are the benefits worth the cost?
- Can you accomplish the same outcome without punishment?

Accidents Have Multiple Causes

A common response to an accident is to find out what caused it and, if it was human behavior, to punish that behavior to ensure it doesn't happen again. This approach has several problems, one of which is that accidents usually have many causes. The root cause process used by one of our clients includes over 200 different possible contributors to be considered when investigating an incident, for example.

With the many ways that things can go wrong, it is unlikely that the cause of an accident can be boiled down to one person's behavior. Most accidents represent the coming together of multiple events or circumstances, any one of which alone would not result in an incident. Unfortunately, in too many cases, despite the multifaceted nature of the event, investigations end in discipline of the frontline employee(s) at the point of the accident. As we will discuss below, this simplistic response rarely has the intended impact.

Furthermore, when other employees see or suspect that the accident has multiple root causes and that some of the blame lies in management-controlled circumstances (hazardous conditions, poor design of equipment, motivation systems, and so on) resentment builds and moves the organization further from a high-performance safety culture.

Effective Punishment

The definition of a punisher is anything that follows behavior that reduces the probability of that behavior in the future. Given this definition, punishment appears to be the right consequence after an incident. If an at-risk behavior causes an accident (or is one of the causes), it is reasonable to want to reduce the probability of that behavior. Yet, using punishment effectively is anything but simple.

Several variables impact the effectiveness of punishment and thus make it difficult to use. First, as with reinforcers, things that are punishing vary widely across people and circumstances, so standardized disciplinary processes are not likely to work universally.

Second, a delay between the undesired behavior and the punisher reduces the punishment's effectiveness. The longer the delay, the weaker the effect. This is one of the reasons that the natural negative consequence from an injury is a better punisher than a reprimand that comes days later. Third, research shows that occasionally punishing undesired behavior is much less effective than punishing many or all instances of the undesired behavior. Thus, when at-risk behavior is occurring often, punishment delivered only when the at-risk behavior causes an incident is too infrequent. As you can see, even when punishment is warranted, it is very difficult to use effectively in a work setting.

Side Effects of Punishment

In addition to the difficulties of executing punishment effectively, one must deal with its predictable negative side effects. To use punishment without considering the side effects is like using thalidomide to reduce morning sickness. It will work, but at what cost?

The side effects of occasional and appropriate use of punishment are mitigated when embedded in a culture of positive reinforcement. Unfortunately, most organizations use too little positive reinforcement to offset the negative side effects of punishment. Listed below are the common side effects of the disproportional use of punishment:

- Lower morale
- Lower productivity
- Decreased teamwork
- Decreased volunteerism
- Increased turnover
- Lower trust
- Desire to retaliate
- Suppressed reporting of incidents, accidents, and near misses

While all these side effects should be of concern, the last one is of critical importance to safety. When people are fearful that reporting an incident, near miss, or even an at-risk behavior will result in punishment, they will not report. Without accurate, honest, and frequent dialogue between hourly workers and management, organizations cannot approach a sustainable, high-performance safety culture.

As consultants we have often witnessed the surprise expressed by management when an incident occurs. The surprise comes from not being in a position to see the circumstances that set up the incident (the coming together of root causes). In many cases the hourly workers are less surprised because they saw the precursors: hazardous conditions that didn't get reported (or got reported but not fixed); employees working beyond the point of fatigue; at-risk behavior patterns in themselves and their peers; antecedents and consequences that encouraged risk-taking, et cetera. Management is not in the work environment enough to observe or experience all of these potential root causes. proactive safety culture requires hourly workers' willingness to discuss the obstacles to safety that they see and experience, but most importantly, a willingness of employees to work together with management to address such obstacles. Punishment suppresses that willingness.

Sidney Dekker, in his book *Just Culture: Balancing Safety and Accountability*, discusses how punishing those involved in accidents and incidents does more damage than good precisely because it leads to fear of reporting and discussing near misses and at-risk behaviors. He describes many situations where valuable information that could have prevented accidents was not brought forward out of fear of punishment. We'll discuss this more later. For now, let's look at why organizations use punishment or feel compelled to use punishment around safety.

Why Companies Do It

In our years in the safety business we have seen a variety of responses to accidents and incidents and a variety of reasons given for those responses. Some of the reasons for using punishment are described on the pages that follow. In the vast majority of cases the response an organization selects has, as its primary goal, ensuring the accident or incident does not happen again. So we shall see, if prevention is the desired outcome, punishment is rarely the right strategy.

REASON 1:
Punishment Provides a Sense of "Doing Something"

A client in the early stages of implementing BBS experienced a rash of incidents. The executive vice president of operations, who was very supportive of BBS and understood the dangers of punishment, finally said, "But I have to do *something* about these incidents!" Our response was, "You are doing something." Using a BBS process to correct the conditions and behaviors that lead to incidents is doing *something*, but it takes time. His response, that it simply didn't feel like he was doing anything, is not unusual. We have heard similar sentiments from other clients. It is unfortunate that a single, decisive, negative action in reaction to an incident is considered to be "doing something" but a plan focused on ensuring the incident will not happen again is not. In reality the plan to strengthen safe work habits will have better and more lasting impact than any disciplinary action ever would. It just doesn't feel like it at the time.

REASON 2:
Using Punishment to Ensure the Performer Doesn't Do It Again

One of the reasons given for using punishment is to make sure the employees directly involved in the incident do not do it again.

We suggest that in the case of injury accidents, the injury itself is usually the best punisher of behavior. As anyone who has suffered a reasonably serious injury because of his/her own behavior can attest, you are very unlikely to do that behavior again. If the pain and suffering is immediate and serious enough, it will function very well to decrease the behavior, and reprimands and suspensions are unnecessary. If the incident does not result in injury, punishment may reduce the performer's tendency to do the behavior again, but is likely to create one or more of the undesirable side effects previously mentioned.

REASON 3:
Using Punishment to Set an Example

Those using punishment often understand that any punishment administered to an injured worker is probably unnecessary, but believe that punishment is important to "send a message" to other employees. It does not seem just to punish someone in order to send a message to others. However, many people believe that not punishing would be to condone the behavior that precipitated the accident. In cases where the performer engaged in blatant and willful violation of policies (in other words, where it is clearly the intent to cause harm) termination is indicated. We will argue later, however, that intention is difficult to determine.

Regardless of whether it is deserved, using punishment to set an example is an attempt to manage the behavior of others through negative reinforcement. The message is, "If you want to avoid punishment, don't do this behavior." We have discussed the limitations of negative reinforcement earlier in this book. Dekker sums up the problem well when he states, "The idea that a charged or convicted practitioner will serve as an example to scare others into behaving more prudently is probably misguided: instead, practitioners will become more careful *only in not disclosing what they have done.*"[1]

REASON 4:
Using Punishment Because Nothing Else Worked

Organizations often believe punishment is required because other attempts to change at-risk behavior have failed. This is not surprising given that most attempts to change at-risk behaviors primarily involve antecedents. This is evidenced by the comments often heard after an incident: "We told them over and over that it is not okay to do this." "The policy is clearly stated in the handbook." "There are signs posted in the area." "We just talked about this in last month's safety meeting." Signs, policies, training, meetings, and discussions are antecedents. Those who do not understand that antecedents will not change behavior permanently are often led to believe that punishment is the only way to "get people's attention." It's not.

REASON 5:
Using Punishment to Demonstrate Action to External Parties

Sometimes punishment is not directed toward behavior change at all, but is simply a way to demonstrate that action has been taken. Serious incidents usually result in a call to action—"What are you going to do about it?" Punishment is sometimes used to show senior management, OSHA, other employees, or family members of injured parties that action has been taken. Punishment looks like a good response. It rarely is. Most concerned parties would be satisfied with a plan detailing how similar incidents will be prevented in the future.

REASON 6:
Using Punishment When Others Call for "Someone to Pay"

Sometimes the call for action is more specific: there is a call for those responsible to "pay for their actions." This is most common when injury or damage has occurred as a result of the incident (someone was hurt or sickened, property or the environment was damaged). Payment aimed at repairing damage may be appropriate. However, if the call for "someone to pay" is aimed at simply punishing the responsible party, what purpose does that serve? If it is to make sure that particular individuals won't do it again, it may or may not work, as we have discussed. If it is to make victims feel better, it is probably not worth the cost. Most importantly, punishment will not ensure the incident won't happen again and isn't that the most important outcome?

Misplaced Accountability

The call to hold someone accountable for an incident is ubiquitous. It is heard after airline accidents, medical errors, environmental disasters, industrial accidents, and even situations such as a country's financial crisis. Accountability is important. As Dekker points out, "Calls for accountability themselves are, in essence, about trust. They are about people, regulators, the public, employees, trusting that you will take problems inside your organization seriously—that you will do something about them, and hold the people responsible for those problems to account."[2]

The question is: Does accountability have to involve punishment?

Virginia Sharpe, in her studies of medical harm, has made an important discrimination between what she calls "forward-looking accountability" and "backward-looking accountability."[3] Backward-looking accountability is about finding blame, finding the individual who made the mistake and delivering punishment. As we have noted earlier, such action may feel good, and may ensure that an individual performer won't make that mistake again, but delivering punishment won't do much else. It won't guarantee that others won't make the mistake and it won't fix any organizational problems that contributed to the incident.

Forward-looking accountability acknowledges the mistake and any harm it caused but, more importantly, it identifies changes that need to be made, and assigns responsibility for making those changes. The accountability is focused around making changes—building safe habits and a safe physical environment—that will prevent a recurrence, not on punishing those who made the mistake.

As noted earlier, investigations usually have as a primary goal ensuring an incident doesn't happen again. However most of the effort is expended on backward-looking accountability. After the investigation is done, the appropriate parties have been disciplined, and any damage repaired, there is often spotty follow-through on the action items identified to prevent a reoccurrence. Concrete action items such as repairing a piece of equipment have a high probability of completion. It is the less-tangible action items such as changing supervisory practices, modifying processes for ensuring better engineering designs, and encouraging peer feedback around behaviors that lead to incidents, for which accountability often falls apart. This is precisely the accountability we believe should be the focus. Holding the appropriate parties accountable for fixing the behavioral conditions that lead to the incident should be of primary concern. Yet, such action is often dropped or done poorly. One act of punishment is easy; ongoing follow-up is not.

Lost Lessons

Organizations are always changing. Technology changes, the equipment changes, the people and their skill level changes, and the pressures and priorities change. This results in ever-changing hazards. A world-class safety process is one where people are responding to those changes and asking (out loud) how accidents might occur and how to prevent them. It is clear that extremely valuable lessons can be learned from near misses, incidents, accidents and at-risk behavior. Yet most organizations struggle to get workers to report near misses and worry about non-reporting of accidents.

Make no mistake: it is the threat of punishment that causes these problems. When people are afraid to discuss mistakes because mistakes too often lead to punishment, then they will not come forward and the lessons will be lost.

Does Lack of Punishment Condone At-Risk Behavior?

As we have said, sometimes punishment is the right thing to do. Blatant, willful violations of safety policies and procedures are probably best handled with punishment. To not punish under such circumstances may indeed condone at-risk behavior. But what about the majority of circumstances that are not so clear-cut, where blame is not so easily assigned? If incidents are resolved without punishment, does that condone any at-risk behavior that may have been involved? We think not. We believe it is possible to clearly communicate that certain at-risk behaviors are unacceptable without the use of punishment. Or, more importantly, we believe it is possible to clearly communicate the criticality of certain *safe behaviors* without the use of punishment.

Priorities are communicated by what management does. When management works to change the antecedents, consequences, and conditions that lead performers to engage in at-risk behavior, a priority is established. When management works with the hourly population to establish effective safety improvements, it sends the message that safety is the priority. Relentless action toward preventing at-risk behavior sends a clear, consistent, and fair message: no punishment required.

Summary

To summarize, the danger of using punishment is that you create a culture of fear and mistrust and that results in people hiding their mistakes and not reporting them so that they and others can learn from them. The tremendous loss of valuable information that could be used to create a safer workforce is a tragedy. The irony is that punishment rarely has the desired impact anyway.

Yet, incidents must be dealt with. We have attempted to show that it is possible to respond to incidents in a behaviorally sound way that will result in lower probability of recurrence. While every incident is different and complex, consider this general approach, which summarizes some of our earlier recommendations:

- Approach the incident by assuming it is a failure of management, not the failure of an individual.

- Conduct an accident investigation and identify all root causes, including the behavioral root causes.

- Conduct a PIC/NIC Analysis® of all identified at-risk behaviors (at all levels).

- Create a plan to remediate all possible root causes as soon as possible, including changes to management practices, organizational systems, et cetera, that may have contributed to at-risk behavior.

- Make the action plan public and highly visible; post it on a bulletin board, for example.

- Create a frequent and public accountability system to complete action items. Assign items to individuals and have those individuals report on progress as a part of regular meetings. Involve senior management in the accountability. Celebrate when action items are complete.

- When action items are complete, update the plan so all can see what has been accomplished and what is yet to be accomplished.

- As action items are completed, management should check back with the performers involved in the incident and/or others performing the same tasks to assess the probability of the same mistake occurring. In other words, have the action items truly changed the behavior?

- Build an ongoing process for checking that the root causes remain addressed.

- Remember, if managers are to change their behavior, positive reinforcement is required to sustain and maintain those changes.

---

[1] Dekker, S. (2007). *Just culture: balancing safety and accountability.* Ashgate Publishing Limited. Burlington, VT. p. 96.

[2] Dekker, S. (2007). *Just culture: balancing safety and accountability.* Ashgate Publishing Limited. Burlington, VT. p. 23.

[3] Sharpe, V. A. (2003). "Promoting patient safety: An ethical basis for policy deliberation." *Hastings Center Report Special Supplement,* 33(5), S1 – S20.

[4] Dekker, S. (2007). *Just culture: balancing safety and accountability.* Ashgate Publishing Limited. Burlington, VT. p. 78.

[5] Reason, J.T. (1997). *Managing the risks of organizational accidents.* Ashgate Publishing Limited, Burlington VT. p. 126.

This article is adapted from: "Safe By Accident? Take the Luck out of Safety: Leadership Practices that Build a Sustainable Safety Culture." Daniels & Agnew (Performance Management Publications 2010).

PERSONAL RESPONSIBILITY WITHIN A BEHAVIORAL APPROACH

Judy Agnew

A behavioral approach to safety focuses on how organizational and management systems influence behavior. The goal is to first look at systems for causes of at-risk behavior, rather than blaming individuals. Some people have trouble reconciling the influence of organizational/management systems on at-risk behavior and the concept of personal responsibility for safety. The question is: if at-risk behavior is found to be influenced by management-controlled organizational systems, does that let the frontline performer off the hook?

To some extent this is a philosophical issue. The notion of personal responsibility is embedded in our culture. It is present in our judicial, political and social systems and has served us well in many respects. In a work setting, telling employees that they are "responsible for their personal safety" at work is helpful as a broad antecedent. It sets the expectation that each person must do what they can to protect themselves and others. The question is what specifically are they responsible for? Telling miners they are responsible for their own safety and then sending them into a mine that is poorly ventilated and structurally unsound is absurd. They cannot be responsible for their own safety under those conditions because they do not control them. We think everyone will agree with this extreme example. The difficulty comes with less extreme examples. Workers who are trained in procedures but don't follow them consistently, for example. Our position is that there is shared responsibility in most cases. Our concern with the notion of "personal responsibility" is that it sounds like an easy solution to a very complex problem. We are sure that some of you have told employees in your organization that they are responsible for their personal safety. We assume since you are reading this, that hasn't solved all your safety problems. Antecedents rarely do.

So where does personal responsibility fit in?

Let's back up. The goal in safety is to prevent injury and illness. If we say that people are responsible for their own safety, then it follows that if they are not safe, they are to blame. Our point is that blaming people for things that are, at least to some extent, outside of their control does not accomplish the goal. If it did more organizations would be perfectly safe by now. But let us be very clear: we are not suggesting that *accountability* (a synonym of responsibility) is bad. Accountability is essential in safety. However, it is critical that organizations first determine WHO should be accountable for WHAT. The word, accountability, is often code for whom to punish. The issue is not who should be punished but what actions will correct the situation so that it will not recur. Although punishment is appropriate under certain circumstances, we see too often that organizations punish only the person at the point of the accident without fully understanding the systemic issues that have contributed. This is not only unjust, but it fails to rectify the situation.

Systems are designed and maintained by people. Therefore, there should be accountability for those who control the systems to change the systems if they are faulty. Once the systems are changed then everyone who works in those systems should be held accountable (positively reinforced for engaging in safe behaviors and corrected when they are not). This is not about absolving personal responsibility—quite the opposite. It is about establishing accountability, at all levels, that will lead to true improvement. Frontline performers need to be held accountable *for those things under their control.* They should be responsible for reporting hazards, providing feedback to keep peers safe, participating in safety meetings, talking to management when systems make working safely more difficult, offering solutions, and working to improve their own safe behaviors. Frontline performers will be more successful in "taking personal responsibility for their safety" if they work in partnership with management and those who control the organizational systems within which they work.

This blog originally appeared on https://www.aubreydaniels.com/blog/2011/10/27/personal-responsibility-within-a-behavioral-approach (updated 2021).

TAKING A SAFETY CULTURE SELFIE

Judy Agnew

Safety is a continuous improvement endeavor. We are never done. It is never enough. Even when organizations have stellar lagging, and leading indicators, we all know that the possibility of an incident still looms. Knowing this is what drives organizations to keep doing more; to keep investing their time and/or resources in ways to make the workplace even safer. Conducting assessments of progress is an important component of continuous improvement. But self-assessments can be difficult and/or misleading.

Natural biases, organizational politics, and simply being unable to see the forest for the trees makes conducting a self-assessment challenging. An outside perspective is helpful. Looking at your safety systems and processes from a different vantage point can illuminate what is working well and should be continued, what isn't working and should be discontinued, and what might be missing that can take your organization to the next level in safety. The science of behavior provides an extremely helpful vantage point from which to view your safety culture and practices. After all, safety is about behavior. We accomplish improvements in safety through a variety of behaviors—for example:

- executives making decisions that support safety,
- supervisors identifying and eliminating hazards,
- EHS professionals providing effective safety training,
- managers giving clear messages about the importance of safe production, and
- frontline performers following safety procedures.

The optimal safety environment requires different behaviors from many different people at all levels of an organization. Conducting a behavioral assessment allows organizations to evaluate the consistency and quality of those critical behaviors and determine how well the organization supports those behaviors over time. Too often organizations fool themselves into thinking that safety behaviors are happening consistently just because they have training, rules, and safety meetings.

A few years ago I experienced a clear example of this when an executive of a large transportation company said to me, "What I want to know is how do we prevent an accident like the one we just had where a guy got hurt because he wasn't wearing his hard hat, and that was the only time he worked without his hard hat in the 15 years he worked for us?" I thought he was kidding. He wasn't. He believed that because wearing hard hats was a rule, and they had disciplinary processes in place, if workers were caught without their hard hats, that meant everyone wore the hats consistently (except this one guy, on this one day). While extreme, this is an example of how a lack of understanding of behavior can blind people from what is really happening and therefore from what improvements they should be focusing on.

The science of behavior has much to teach us, but there are two lessons in particular that will help you look at your safety management system from a different vantage point:

- Behavior is a function of consequences, not antecedents.

- Immediate and certain consequences are much more powerful than future and uncertain consequences.

These may sound like simple concepts, but this shift in vantage point will make a significant difference (and simple isn't necessarily easy). An assessment conducted by someone trained in behavioral science can help you assess:

- The effectiveness of your training, communications, meetings, and other antecedents

- What behaviors your measurement systems, incentive systems, and other organizational systems are really driving
- How leader behavior is impacting frontline behavior (intentionally and unintentionally)
- The degree of engagement at the frontline and management levels
- What stage your company is in terms of safety culture improvement

Whether you are planning to make improvements, in the middle of a new initiative, or wrapping up some change effort, applying a behavioral lens to take stock of where you are will help you see gaps and opportunities that you might not otherwise see, and it will help ensure that your improvement efforts pay off.

This blog originally appeared on https://www.aubreydaniels.com/blog/taking-safety-culture-selfie (updated 2021).

WHY RELATIONSHIPS MATTER IN SAFETY

Judy Agnew

Have you ever noticed how supervisors who have good relationships with their crews tend to have safer crews? In fact, good relationships tend to be associated with all kinds of good performance. Why would this be so? What do relationships have to do with safety?

The link is discretionary effort. Discretionary effort is that effort which employees can give at work, but don't have to. Discretionary effort is going above the basic requirements, and it rarely occurs in the context of poor employee-management relationships. Many people think of safety as a compliance issue—getting people to comply with safety rules, regulations, and procedures. However, if you want to go beyond compliance and create a high-performance safety culture, discretionary effort is a requirement. Truly exceptional safety requires that people don't just follow procedures, comply with OSHA standards, and wear personal protective equipment (PPE). Exceptional safety happens when people look for and report hazards, give peers feedback on safe and at-risk behavior, and most difficult of all, admit when they have made mistakes (report near misses) so lessons can be learned. You don't get this kind of engagement in safety when employees dislike, distrust, and (most importantly) fear their boss. If people think being honest about a safety infraction will lead to reprimands and discipline, then they won't be open and honest. In other words, you won't get discretionary effort.

Discretionary effort is created through the use of positive reinforcement. Research shows that when people are recognized for what they do well around safety and when reporting problems and concerns is met with reinforcing consequences (such as joint problem solving and problem resolution), employees will be more engaged in safety.

So what does discretionary effort and positive reinforcement have to do with relationships? Positive reinforcement is disabled by poor relationships. Not only are people less willing to use positive reinforcement within the context of a poor relationship, but when they do, that reinforcement is less effective. If you tell someone they've done a good job and/or try to show concern for their safety, but they dislike you and therefore don't care what you think, your attempts at reinforcement are less likely to be effective.

Having a good relationship doesn't mean being nice all the time or being soft on safety. Good relationships at work include accountability and constructive feedback. They are also not about being friends with direct reports or being someone they want to go to a ball game with. A positive relationship isn't necessarily about your personality characteristics. In other words, you don't have to be outgoing, overly friendly, or the life of the party to establish yourself as a sincere, positive, and fair manager or leader. Positive employee-management relationships include mutual trust and respect as a foundation for a partnership around safety or any other optimal job performance.

So how does a boss develop a good relationship with direct reports? Listed below are behaviors that consistently contribute to positive workplace relationships. These behaviors can be exhibited by any "personality type" and can lead to improvements in safety and work in general.

Best Practices for Building Effective Relationships around Safety

Set clear expectations.
- Use pinpointed (actionable) words to ensure clarity of expectations; avoid assumptions and ask recipient(s) to state an understanding of the expectations.

Listen.

- Use active listening skills such as maintaining eye contact, using appropriate facial expressions, paraphrasing, and asking questions to demonstrate understanding. Avoid looking at or using computers and smart phones when others are talking to you.

Acknowledge good work, not just mistakes/problems.

- Track the nature of your interactions. Good leaders maintain a higher ratio of positive to constructive comments/discussions.

Ask questions to understand problems/issues.

- Avoid jumping to conclusions. There is always more to every story. Ask questions to uncover the details.

Ask for feedback about your own effectiveness and areas for improvement.

- Seek detailed information about what you do well and what you need to do differently to be more effective.
- Demonstrate that you are listening and working to improve your own actions.

Avoid blame.

- People's behavior makes sense to them, even if it doesn't make sense to you. Find out what antecedents and consequences were in place that led to undesired behavior.

Respond fairly to incidents (safety and other types).

- Better incident investigations will lead to fair responses.

Admit when you make mistakes.

- Acknowledging your own mistakes helps establish that mistakes are expected and that learning from them is critical.

Solicit input and opinions from direct reports.

- Asking for input and advice will not only lead to better solutions, but in many cases, it also demonstrates respect.

Follow through on commitments.

- Consistent follow-through is essential for building trust and respect. Use whatever memory devices you need to be sure to do what you say you will do.

Stand up for direct reports; "go to bat" for them.

- Verbally promote direct reports and share their successes with others. In addition, acknowledge some responsibility when direct reports make mistakes.

Remove roadblocks in order to set up direct reports for success.

- The number-one job of management is to make direct reports successful. Analyze what gets in their way and do what you can to remove obstacles.

Provide feedback that helps direct reports improve.

- Pinpointed, timely feedback is most helpful. Don't save feedback for annual appraisals or even monthly one-on-one meetings; just-in-time feedback is the most effective.

Demonstrate that you trust direct reports.

- Give employees appropriate responsibilities and avoid micromanaging. When appropriate, tell them you trust them, and reinforce trustworthy behaviors.

Treat direct reports like people, not just employees.

- Make a point to greet direct reports at the start of the shift (when possible); show an interest in their lives outside of work, and demonstrate concern and consideration.

Clearly, these so-called "soft skills" are well worth developing if you want to create relationships that result in a trusting and thus high-performance safety culture.

This article originally appeared on https://www.aubreydaniels.com/media-center/why-relationships-matter-safety (updated 2021).

COMBATTING THE RARE ERROR

Aubrey Daniels

Organizational operations are increasingly complex. As a result, keeping workers and the environment safe is becoming equally complex. Common sense and decades-old approaches are no longer enough. A truly safe work environment requires executives, managers and frontline workers who understand their own and each other's behavior and how to create an environment where even rare errors are anticipated and planned for.

The way an organization handles rare errors is a litmus test for how well leaders understand behavior as it relates to safety. Rare errors are often approached as individual or group failures, when in fact they are most often a failure of leadership.

There are usually two causes of rare errors. They are caused by inadequate training or by an environment that produces too few reinforcers to keep the employee focused on the task. By *focused* we mean that the performer is immune to elements in the environment that would tend to distract him.

Fluency Training and The Rare Error

In order to execute a process or procedure safely, one must know how to do a task safely and have the motivation to perform it exactly as trained. *Behavior fluency* is defined as automatic, non-hesitant responding. Its benefits are long-term retention of skills and knowledge, improved attention span, resistance to distraction, endurance, and application of the knowledge and skill to novel situations. The advantages of fluency to safety are obvious; however, safety training rarely reaches fluency and many organizations depend on long periods of on-the-job experience to reach it. The problem is that during the long period where habits are not at the fluency level, exposure is unnecessarily high.

The investment in training to fluency has a very large payback when all the costs of accident and injury are factored into the safety equation. As T.C. Cumming, a former Navy Seal says, "The more you sweat in times of peace, the less you bleed in times of war." He is referring to the intense training that Navy Seals undergo in order to perform flawlessly on their missions. Many accidents and injuries are due to inadequate training in that fluency was not demonstrated at the point of training. By not training to fluency, we save a penny that will later cost us a dollar . . . or much more.

Extinction: The Unseen Obstacle in Safety

Extinction is the decrease in the frequency of behavior caused by a lack of reinforcement. In other words, without reinforcement behavior fades away. Although many factors affect the rate of extinction, in general the rate is related to the number of reinforcers received for the behavior. Behaviors that receive few reinforcers in training and few on the job are subject to the effects of extinction in a matter of days or even hours. The following graph demonstrates that behaviors that receive fewer reinforcers extinguish more quickly.

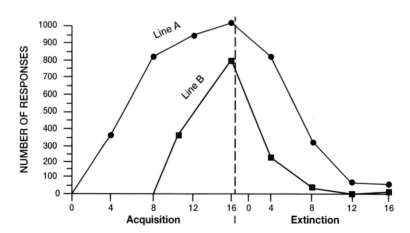

Representation of extinction curves as a function of number of reinforcers. Subjects on **Line A** received twice as many reinforcers as ones on **Line B**. Extinction on Line B occurs quicker. For more on extinction see Millenson (1967), Hantula and Crowell (1994) and Daniels and Daniels (2004).

Increased Risk of Catastrophic Failure

An irony in safety is that the better you get at working safely, the higher the risk you run for having a catastrophic failure. As safety performance improves, there will be fewer reinforcers for monitoring behavior. Therefore, when an incident does occur, it has the potential to be catastrophic; no one will be looking because looking will likely have undergone extinction.

An early sign that extinction is occurring is that small variances in usual performance occur, but are not thought to be significant. These variances may take the form of misreading a dial or gage, not paying attention to an unusual noise, being preoccupied with some off-task situation, or failing to make a periodic check of equipment. In time, these variances will occur much more frequently since "not doing something" requires less effort, a built-in reinforcer. Since attending is less frequent over time, the catastrophic event will catch everyone off guard when it occurs.

Job focus is determined by the frequency of reinforcers received. When the majority of the reinforcers available in a job setting come from doing the work, employees are highly focused on the job. When few reinforcers are produced by focusing on the work, it takes very little non-work activity to distract any performer—a sign of impending extinction.

From a leadership perspective, small variances in safety performance always demand attention since they may be an indication of extinction, the unseen danger in a high-performing safety culture.

Methods for Protecting Against the Rare Error

When you observe employees in the workplace, you will see what is and is not reinforcing. Whatever people are doing pinpoints where the reinforcement is occurring. If employees are focused on the job, reinforcement is occurring for those work behaviors. If people are looking around, checking social media on their cell phones, chatting with a colleague, or just daydreaming, you know that insufficient reinforcement is taking place to keep people focused on their tasks.

This knowledge is highly diagnostic for safety leaders as they can see potential problems that relate not only to safety but to areas such as productivity and quality. When employees are not on task, there is a problem with the rate of reinforcement available for the performer on that task. When you understand this fact, it is easy to see that punishing the performer will not solve the problem. Unless actions are taken to increase reinforcement for the task, attention to the task will decrease and eventually extinction will occur.

Because of the high levels of quality and safety in some organizations, the behavior of checking for errors or problems produces no reinforcement for the observer since their job (reinforcer) is to catch the error. Therefore some method of creating things to catch, see or respond to is needed to sustain high levels of checking performance.

TSA screeners at airports, for example, look at large numbers of briefcases, suitcases, and so on without finding suspicious items. The solution is for TSA to put more items in the system and reinforce improvement in catching them, not to take the performers off the line for more training. In this case training is not the problem. The behavior is extinguished on the line and that is the only place that the error can be corrected.

Many performers go through safety checks and inspections overlooking errors in plain sight. This is not because they are lazy or careless but because the environment they work in has insufficient reinforcers to maintain high levels of alertness. It is the leader's responsibility to engineer those environments to produce effective levels of reinforcement. Therefore, the employee's behavior is a reflection of how well the leader is doing his/her job.

Knowing the science of behavior in detail produces solutions to many problems that have plagued organizations for a very long time. Granted, common-sense solutions work sometimes, but often they don't. Conversely, the laws of behavior never change. Once you know them you are able to solve problems in a new and ever-changing workplace.

This article originally appeared on www.forbes.com (updated 2021).

NEW-HIRE TRAINING: BEHAVIORAL APPROACH CAN LEAD TO SIGNIFICANT TRAINING ROI

Tom Spencer

Costs associated with onboarding new employees often go well beyond initial training to include weeks or even months of "learning on the job." This is especially true when the initial training focuses on general orientation information not linked to what the employees will be paid to do and accomplish. Training that doesn't directly improve workplace performance is a waste of time and money. Organizations that use a behavioral approach to training ensure a streamlined focus on what matters to the organization and what will directly impact business results.

What does a behavioral approach to training look like?

Training developed to cover critical content is the first step. Trainers often pack so much information into training that the participants have difficulty figuring out what they "need-to-know" versus what is "nice-to-know." Content must be applicable only to how the employee does his or her job, which may also include how and when they interact with other individuals or departments.

Practice, Practice, Practice!

Training that incorporates meaningful practice and application will greatly increase the opportunity for the employee to learn, retain and act on what's really important for them to do or do differently in their job. By simulating real-life situations, employees can put themselves in the job and understand how their decision-making will lead them to the most safe and productive outcome.

Reinforce the right behavior in the workplace.

A behavioral approach to training will not be enough unless the right consequences are built into the natural work environment. Consequences must support the skills trained. The behavior gets started in the classroom but it's only through measurement, feedback and reinforcement that the desired behavior will keep going in the workplace. The result is performance mastery and fluency that accelerates your overall business and safety performance.

Case Study

Take for example, a medical insurance company that was in need of streamlining its new-hire training for underwriters, claims processors, and call center representatives. Their current training program, primarily lecture-based, was costly to implement and delivering mixed results. The company invested in integrating a behavioral approach to training by redesigning three new-hire courses, building fluency in key job tasks, and developing a plan to measure the impact of the redesign on job performance. In addition, they developed a core group of internal staff to be skilled in course redesign and fluency-based learning so they could take ownership of training going forward.

The training redesign process refocused on the primary job tasks and the knowledge required to perform those tasks correctly and without hesitation (fluently). The redesign replaced much of the lecture format of the existing courses with hundreds to thousands of opportunities to practice components of the critical job tasks in a way that produced accuracy and speed in the full job tasks. The learning format included traditional classroom instruction, online knowledge fluency training, computer system drills, and job task and process drills that required the integrated use of medical knowledge, online resources, computer applications, and communication skills.

The design and development of each of the courses required coordination and communication with internal stakeholder groups (e.g.,

Human Resources, operations, nursing staff) and a review of and revisions to the online resources that supported the job positions addressed.

Student progress was tracked with individual scorecards that summarized their performance on classroom exercises and tests. Students also charted their accuracy and speed of responding for each practice exercise so they could monitor their performance improvement. At the end of each day, the instructor reviewed the students' charts and performance scorecards.

*The intended results of each course redesign were to reduce the length of the new-hire training, better align the course content with the job process, and increase the amount and relevance of the practice so that new hires would perform as well as seasoned employees more quickly than they had in the past. **Actual results from the redesign of the underwriting course alone yielded a reduction in classroom training time by 15 days (or 34%), a reduction in post-training time from 26 to 3 weeks, a 43% improvement in After Call Wrap (ACW) performance, and significant improvement in Quality Assessment Scores of new hires in the first 5 weeks post-training.***

Fluency techniques can and should be applied to all essential training. Safety, customer service, and quality training all benefit from instructional design focused on building fluency of critical skills. Organizations can save time, money, and in the case of safety, potentially lives by adopting these powerful techniques.

This article is adapted from: "New-Hire Training," Aubrey Daniels International, https://www.aubreydaniels.com/media-center/new-hire-training.

NEAR-MISS REPORTING:
BEST PRACTICES FROM BROWN-FORMAN

Bart Sevin

The value of a good Near-Miss Reporting System is clear. When well-executed, such systems not only help maintain a safe physical environment, they also build engagement, trust, and improve communication. Two years ago, with the help of Aubrey Daniels International (ADI), Brown-Forman, makers of famous brands such as Jack Daniel's, Old Forester, and Sonoma-Cutrer, embarked on a behavioral safety journey. In the Stevenson Mill, they applied what they learned about behavior to build a more robust Near-Miss Reporting System. ADI Senior Consultant Bart Sevin, who has worked with all of the Brown-Forman sites, talked with Howard Burcham, Mill Manager, and Dan Parker, Maintenance Manager and BBS Site Champion, to hear firsthand about what they did that led to their success.

SEVIN: What was it specifically that prompted your work to improve near-miss reporting at Stevenson?

BURCHAM: Four years ago our facility had 12 injuries. Three years ago we had 5. Two years ago we had 2. Last year we had none. If we went from 12 to none in one year I would be less impressed than I am by our true *journey*. I have been in manufacturing for 30 years. One question that has always troubled me is, "How can we manage our safety?" I had watched facilities (some that I was a part of) hit milestones in safety to only exhale and regress backwards, often times having injuries again. It's the kind of thing that wakes me up at night. I couldn't answer the question, "What can my team do to manage their safety and not just be lucky?" My goal was to be able to point precisely to the reasons for our success if asked how we did it. The Near-Miss Program is something we can point to. We always say that team members have the power to stop the plant operations for an unsafe condition or act. The Near-Miss Program gives them the power to run the plant safely. This system provides an avenue for our team to point out (and even fix on their own) things in our plant that cause unsafe conditions or acts.

SEVIN: Stevenson casts its net a bit wider than is typical, so how do you define a near miss?

BURCHAM: One thing that has made a difference for us is identifying upset conditions as precursors to near misses. These are usually seen as throughput or production issues, not safety issues. But we realized that upset conditions often lead to risk and are therefore important for near-miss reporting. Traditionally near misses might be something like a puddle on the floor, but we ask our people to think further upstream and now the operator writes up things that caused the puddle in the first place. Another example is a seam in a conveyor that causes product to jam and stop the line. To un-jam the line, the operator must use his LOTO locks, alternative LOTO (interlocks), and a crow bar to clear the jam. There are a lot of potential injuries in that process. If we start by fixing the seam issue, there is no possibility of a jam. Our motto is, "The operator is at his/her safest standing there doing the job—anything else exposes them to risks."

SEVIN: What suggestions do you have for the reporting process itself? How do you make it as simple as possible for people to escalate a near miss?

BURCHAM: First and foremost, I think organizations over-think the process. It's best to make the forms readily available in an area like the break room. We recognize that some people are shy; they don't want to hand it to their supervisor. Others are willing to hand it to a supervisor but they shouldn't have to chase one down. Make it easy. Have a place for the employee to drop the form off and then check it often! If parts need to be ordered just let the employee know and keep moving. Some plants want to meet two or three times with the employee and engineering and make a lengthy, detailed process out of it. Life is busy. Often there isn't time for all the formality and it leads to unnecessary delays. Getting things fixed quickly is important. A great example of that is last year one of our employees turned in a form at 7:00 a.m. I picked up the form at 7:15 from the tray in the break room. Dan (maintenance manager) fixed it at lunch. At 3:30 p.m. the employee said, "Someone else must have already turned in the Near Miss I did this morning." I asked him why he thought that. He said, "It was fixed so quickly." I told him, "No one else reported it. We got your form and fixed it, that's all." There is no need for formal close out meetings with a panel of people. Trust me, if you fix their Near Miss they will notice and it spreads from there.

SEVIN: You mentioned that you once had everyone look for sharp edges after a near miss at another mill. Are there any other group activities like this you have done around near misses?

BURCHAM: As of today we have gone 365 working days with no injuries! I monitor the other plant's First Aid and Near Miss entries to capture trends or "targets" we can check against our own facility. It can range from machine guarding issues, wiring, you name it! If anyone else has seen something, it could easily be here at Stevenson as well. I also look at what I call "nags;" nagging items like, "I always have to monitor the gates at the machines to make sure the tool tight guarding is in place." We put this out in the morning meeting for everyone to check. We do "wall-to-wall" inspections where we grab a couple of people and give them a few items to check and let them cover the plant wall-to-wall looking at these items. We also have to do biweekly environmental walks of the entire property for EPA compliance. I always have the inspectors carry a handful of Near Miss Forms. We have done "360" inspections where I will have a team with Near Miss Forms go completely around the outside of the building 360 degrees and look for safety or environmental issues.

SEVIN: There is a reward of sorts at the end of each month for employees who submit near misses, but what are the positive reinforcers (R+) for reporting near misses besides the bottle they may be awarded?

BURCHAM: Honestly we have very few formal meetings. We stop at the employee's workstation and update them on a form they filled out, but nothing formal. The poker chip is the cornerstone of the program. Team members receive a poker chip for every Near Miss Form turned in. It is worth roughly a dollar and is redeemed for company merchandise from our company store. We also have a competition between sister plants. The plant with the most forms submitted wins the "Gold:" a bottle of Jack Daniel's No 27 Gold. It is fairly rare and retails for $150.00. We raffle this off to a lucky team member if our plant wins. Some people only turn in one form or so a month and some turn in dozens. The more that are turned in the better your raffle chances (our plants are small so the chances of winning are pretty good). We have one employee who turns in dozens a month and she redeems her poker chips for shirts and other clothing so she does not have to buy work clothes. But the real value in the poker chip is that it gives us the opportunity to open up a conversation about their Near Miss Form or anything else they might want to talk about. In the beginning I did more coaching and maybe even allowed a Near Miss Form on some very low priority stuff but the seeds needed to be planted and built from there. I still get a lot of people that come up and say, "I don't know if this is a Near Miss or not." or "Is this a Near Miss?" I have never rejected one. I may have to coach or "lead" them into a better or different version of what they have questioned, but I never reject it. Growing up, my Dad always said you may not like how a new dog trees a squirrel but if you mistreat him and don't train him you'll be treeing squirrels yourself (not that our team is a bunch of dogs)!" In my opinion, this is the best way to get employee engagement. The average rank and file employee feels like they have no power. This empowers them to actually help run and change things. It's easy for managers to overlook that.

SEVIN: What suggestions do you have for other companies looking to find success with their Near-Miss Reporting Systems?

BURCHAM: When you use something tangible, like the poker chip, remember it's not really about the poker chip but the conversation it allows. I have seen plants making grand presentations with the poker chips and making a big deal of the Near Miss Form but I have found if I go up to someone, hand them the poker chip and strike up a conversation I gain so much more. The military uses "challenge coins" much the same way. It may only be worth a dollar but it breaks the ice and creates a relationship. I also believe it is important to have casino grade chips. They have heft; they clink and clank in your hand. People can easily collect and not lose them. You want those coins to mean something and you make that happen through the conversation you have. That silly little poker chip—worth a dollar—gives us so many opportunities to give social positive reinforcement.

PARKER: It is also important to acknowledge that the process puts more work on maintenance personnel. In order to give encouragement and appreciation, Howard purchased small items (e.g., hats, shirts, hoodies) as reinforcers for the maintenance personnel. This also helped to encourage operators to correct small things on their own. They get two poker chips instead of one when they do this so they can really rack up the chips and purchase what they want, even sooner.

SEVIN: What impact has your Near-Miss Reporting System had?

BURCHAM: The two years before we introduced the Near Miss system we had 0 Near Misses turned in and had 5 and 12 injuries respectively. The first year we introduced it we had about 200 Near Misses reported and 2 injuries. This past year we have addressed over 1,900 Near Misses and have had ZERO Injuries. I believe one of the fastest ways to impact engagement and morale is to have a robust safety program. It breeds pride in the facility and it empowers the team members to manage and run it themselves. It is a short leap to improved productivity and higher morale leads to lower absenteeism. Our Near-Miss System has become an important part of our safety program.

This article is adapted from: "Brown-Forman: Near-Miss Reporting Best Practices," Aubrey Daniels International, https://www.aubreydaniels.com/media-center/near-miss-reporting-best-practices-brown-forman.

CLARK PACIFIC'S SAFETY JOURNEY

Gail Snyder

High-rise hotels, hospitals, stadiums, student housing, churches, casinos, parking garages, all with an artistic flair: these are a few examples of the hundreds of structures that stand as the legacy of Clark Pacific, based in West Sacramento, California. This family business of over half a century specializes in producing and building with state-of-the-art concrete architectural and structural precast materials. A seven year construction project—the new, stellar Apple headquarters in Cupertino, California—is but one visual example of the quality products that come from Clark Pacific's years of service and expertise.

"We have the experience and wisdom of a 50-year-old company with the mentality and enthusiasm of a start-up," said Steve Voss, a 25-year employee and plant manager of the NorCal plant located in Woodland, California (one of three of the organization's manufacturing facilities). Another major and continual project that began in earnest approximately one and a half years ago proves his point. That project is an approach to safety called Safety Leadership.

Until 2015, safety at Clark Pacific was, of course, a very important factor in day-to-day operations. But as Voss explained, "Even though our incident rate was below industry standards, that's just not good enough. We knew we needed to do better. People were getting hurt and that's unacceptable."

Enter Audra Owens, now Director of Environmental, Health and Safety, who had in a previous position come across the book *Safe by Accident? Leadership Practices that Build a Sustainable Safety Culture*—a behavior-based approach to safe workplaces. The book, written by Judy Agnew and Aubrey Daniels of Aubrey Daniels International (ADI), impressed Owens, a safety professional of 20 years. "That book sparked a whole different way of thinking about how to approach safety," Owens explained. She brought this vision with her to Clark Pacific, when one of the first steps she took was to have Bob Clark, President of Operations, read *Safe by Accident*.

A phrase on the book's cover, "Take the luck out of safety," resonated with Clark. He admits that his previous role in the company's safety effort had been to hire safety personnel and remain available to them for consultation when necessary. "We had some good years with safety and our lost-time accidents. I just always knocked on wood when we were having a good year," he said. "I've come a long, long way from there. I realized, like anything, if you want to do it, you've got to put your head down and work hard. It's not about luck; it's about a focused effort to come up with a good solution. With safety, it's a journey. You're never going to get to the end. Even though you might be doing great right now, you can get better. There's something you can do every day to get better at it."

Safety Leadership

Safety Leadership is a positive approach designed to improve leader skills in changing safety-related behavior and promote safety engagement. It involves three general steps. First, identify important safety behaviors at all levels of the organization that will result in improvement. Second, strengthen those behaviors through daily, positive coaching interactions called touchpoints. Third, refine and improve coaching and positive reinforcement use through weekly accountability and debrief meetings. The process ensures everyone at every level is working in concert to achieve targeted safety results. At Clark Pacific, led by Owens and Bart Sevin, senior ADI consultant, the company identified four types of incidents to target first: hand and finger injuries, back injuries, live load violations (exposure of any body part under suspended loads), and crush-point violations. Simultaneously, they worked on increasing near-miss reporting in order to increase organizational learning.

Through much hard work, Owens and the Safety Review Council (SRC) designed a near-miss reporting system using (among other elements) a newly created, pocket-sized notebook containing specific but easy guidelines for reporting near misses. In the months to follow, Owens, who is recognized by everyone on the team as key to the success of the safety process, worked to develop an intranet system that consolidated and shared near-miss reports, incident rates, and other integral information regarding the safety effort. "Safety is a team sport," says Clark. "But having a great leader like Audra makes a lot of difference."

Getting Started

When Owens joined Clark Pacific she began with analysis of the safety activities and culture and conducted extensive interviews at every employee level. "I found there was no consistency and that told me we had a lot to do in building a safety culture," she said. One question that she asked was, "Do you believe that all incidents and injuries are preventable?" The responses surprised her. "A very few people said, 'Yes. I believe that,'" she commented. "Steve Voss was one of them." And according to Voss, so was his assistant plant manager, Frank Kliewer. "He and I were singularly focused," said Voss. "If you ask Frank if all injuries are preventable, he'll beat me to it saying yes."

After Owens and plant safety champions Voss and Brad Williams, Southern California plant manager, attended a one-week, ADI class in Atlanta, they returned with added enthusiasm. "We took away a much broader understanding and application of all things behavior, understanding compliant level versus discretionary effort and what that science can unlock," said Voss.

The next step was having Sevin train 57 leaders in the methods of behavioral safety leadership. Brief one-on-one, safety-focused interactions with direct reports called coaching touchpoints, are now part of the daily routine. At all levels, these brief discussions focus on providing feedback and recognition for the safety critical behaviors identified in the first stage of implementation. In regular meetings, from the top down, leaders conduct debriefs with their direct reports regarding their touchpoints and how they can all work to improve their coaching impact. In addition, weekly "toolbox talks" (company-wide communications to frontline employees regarding selected safe behaviors), and "safety moments" are now a mainstay at all of the Clark Pacific sites. This information is accessible along with the near-miss data on the company intranet Safety Incident Reporting Tracker (SIRT) system.

The Near-Miss System

Clark compares the changed approach to safety and the safety culture to turning a large ship while Voss points out that top leadership absolutely must be on board to accomplish that goal. One of Owens' first steps in doing just that was to create a successful near-miss reporting system. She explained, "If you don't have a robust near-miss program, you're missing the boat, because you will never know what your problems are and what you need to fix."

The near-miss reporting system has definitely become robust—supported by a positive culture change that rewards rather than punishes such reporting. Acknowledging that the drive toward incident prevention takes time in everyone's busy day, Voss and other safety champions regularly consult with supervisors in the plants and field to hone the process. Recently the safety team developed a cell phone app for near-miss reporting. "We eliminated administrative time and the data is there in real time," Voss said. "This, as part of our SIRT system, also helps us quickly respond to real-time metrics and that goes to reinforcing in a more immediate way."

One of many examples where the safety leadership coaching process helped accelerate adoption of important safety-related behaviors was, in fact, around the near-miss system. Frank Kliewer, who reports directly to Voss, utilized coaching touchpoints and debrief meetings to drive near-miss reporting with his direct reports, who in turn used touchpoints to increase the number of near misses reported by their employees. According to Sevin, "Frank is one of many excellent practitioners of the safety leadership coaching process, and he provided an early example of how more effective coaching can be used to drive key safety behaviors—like reporting the near misses that Clark Pacific needed to help move the safety culture in the desired direction."

Benchmarking Results

Many at Clark Pacific mention the change that must take place to emphasize and manage behavior rather than safety results. Today celebrations are held for meeting behavioral milestones (rather than lack of incidents), and that change has brought about significant results. "We're striving for a self-directed workforce, an accident-free workplace," Voss said. "Get past the mindset that an incident is just human error. That's a very convenient, yet shallow root cause, and numbers (lagging indicators) represent real people who have gotten injured."

Clark Pacific participates in a benchmarking group as one of five non-competitive precast concrete companies in the country. The groups meet and exchange information and best practices on a variety of issues in such areas as production, quality, finance, human resources, and, of course, safety. Clark Pacific recently hosted a tour of their facilities for their benchmarking partners which included an overview of their Safety Leadership program followed by actual involvement in the process.

"They were blown away because we showed the inverse correlation between near-miss reporting and our incident rate, and how it's gone based on where we were and where we've come," Voss explained. Between 2015 and 2016, near-miss reports rose by 503 percent while injuries decreased by 78 percent. "You see that correlation and it sells itself!" said Voss.

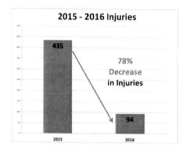
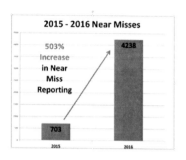

A Culture of Communication

Increased communication, data collection, feedback, and the regular message and activities from the top down that safety comes before any other consideration—all are changing the culture at Clark Pacific. Owens, Voss, and Clark can't express enough the importance of leadership involvement and visible support in making this a successful initiative. "We put a feather in Bob Clark's cap for getting people at all levels involved," said Sevin. "He played a key role because he demonstrated the importance of the process by participating at his level on a consistent basis, and that's critical."

"Messaging is important," Owens said. "We're very much about meaningful and very deliberate communication around safety. We've branded 'One Company. One Life. Zero Injury.' as our logo. I think when you have a passion and believe in this, others get on board when they see that it really makes a difference."

Voss added, "Almost to a person, people are talking in a different language here. In my mind, that's an affirmation that we're seeing the culture change."

The Journey

The people at Clark Pacific have come to the realization that safety is a never-ending effort, or as they often call it, "an ongoing journey." Safety isn't a box that can be checked off as finished, or a number that is satisfied with compliance to industry standards. Safety is about people and people are about behavior.

"The science of human behavior doesn't change," observed Voss. "What are you doing to ensure people will do the right thing even when you're not there? In my opinion, this is the absolute best way to do it."

Clark Pacific is planning to use these same methods in other areas such as quality. "We're now understanding that the behavioral concepts don't just apply to safety," said Clark. "They apply to everything we're doing here. It's changed our culture. The big change for me personally is I realize this is my job, not just a token effort. I realize what we're accomplishing and it's one of the better things that I am doing in this company. The bottom line is that we really want our people safe and going home to their families the way they came to work. It's the moral thing to do and the behavioral science behind it...I believe in it!"

How has Safety Leadership contributed to the safety process at Clark Pacific?

"At our Fontana Plant, the Safety Leadership process as taught and followed correctly has allowed us to flow, like irrigation water, safety down to the line workers. In the past, much of the safety knowledge and learning stopped or was damned at the foreman/lead man level. The line workers often saw safety as a burden to getting their job done. Now those at the end of the row are getting all the water (information and practices water) and are growing. The workers appreciate the way safety is taught and shown to them through touchpoints and the debrief meetings are great for reinforcing and teaching the supervisors the right way to encourage safe practices."

—Brad Williams, Plant Manager

This article is adapted from: "Clark Pacific's Safety Journey," Aubrey Daniels International, https://www.aubreydaniels.com/media-center/clark-pacific-safety-journey.

MAKING SAFETY HAZARD SCANS
REAL-TIME HABITS

Cloyd Hyten

There are many factors to consider when it comes to evaluating and improving your safety culture. Having the right tools and established processes, particularly around hazard recognition, are important ways to prevent injury and near-hit incidents at your company.

Safety Hazard Scans (hereafter called safety scans) are procedures workers can do at the job site to control their personal safety in the face of job hazards present at the beginning of a work task (those hazards that cannot be eliminated entirely by management "standing hazards") or job hazards that emerge only once work is underway ("emerging hazards"). Safety scans are something anyone can do anywhere for any kind of task, so they are one of the few universal injury prevention procedures. Safety scans are designed to enhance situation awareness[1] and prompt workers to take actions to reduce injury risk during a work task. Safe Work Permits, if "walked down" properly, typically incorporate a safety scan of some kind, but permits are not required for every kind of job, so many companies require safety scans as a routine practice.

Safety scans add one more layer of protection onto existing hazard controls. Because they are completed in the task environment, workers can look for the actual, specific hazards in the immediate area. For example, workers may know about potential line-of-fire hazards generally but looking at the task environment at the time of work lets you see the actual line of fire and identify safe zones where workers can stand or walk to avoid the line of fire. Workers judge whether the hazard controls present for this work (engineering controls such as barriers, interlocks, alarms, administrative controls such as their training for the job, safe work procedures, tools and equipment, and, finally, PPE) will keep them safe enough to proceed with the job.

Safety scans go by different names (e.g., field level risk assessment, take two) and different formats, but all share some version of the following steps:

- Pause and ask yourself or discuss with co-workers, "How could I get hurt doing this task?"
  - Look for hazards in the task, the nearby physical environment, the equipment to be used, and the people doing the task or those nearby.
- "What do I need to do to keep me safe when completing this task?"
  - For example, the worker may have to follow the prescribed safe work procedure, communicate with co-workers at critical steps, deviate from the expected procedure to an alternative safe work procedure, etc.
- If there is no safe way to do the task, the worker should stop work and ask for help from supervision or management. Hazard scans without a stop work policy in place are incomplete; they leave the workers no option but to proceed with the task even if they think it is unsafe to do so.
- Remain alert to emerging hazards once the work task is underway. If such hazards arise, re-scan to decide how best to proceed. This step means that scanning does not end pre-task, so calling the whole procedure a "pre-task scan" is misleading.

Management Engagement with Safety Scans

It is management's responsibility to provide a safe workplace overall, but because all risk cannot be removed, they must help workers get better at spotting and handling residual hazards on the job. If we view doing safety scans as a sophisticated human skill, it is apparent that safety scanning needs management support to begin and to maintain at high quality over time just like other safety-critical behaviors. Training is needed at first to teach the fundamentals of hazard recognition based on the hazards likely to be encountered for the nature of the work, as well as using the particular scanning procedure itself, including how to use the stop work policy if needed.

Beyond initial training, to make this tool as effective as possible, additional strengthening should come via coaching interactions from supervision to frontline workers. This kind of post-training coaching is essential to make safety scans a personal habit and a part of the company culture. Here are 4 things supervisors can do to build and maintain high-quality safety scans in the field:

1. When onsite with a work crew, lead them through a scan, or observe and coach their scan.

2. During or after the task, ask questions about the scan, such as, "What hazards did you spot during your safety scan? What did you decide to do about them to keep you safe?"

3. Compliment the good catches and good safety adjustments to reinforce them. Offer constructive feedback for any weak spots you observe directly or hear about in your coaching interaction to prevent the quality from deteriorating.

4. Examine the hazards that workers report in this process and decide whether they should be remediated at a management level rather than dealt with ad hoc in safety scans time after time. If workers see that management takes action against chronic or systemic hazards, that will be a powerful reinforcer for doing safety scans and discussing them with their supervisors.[2]

The re-scanning step of a safety scan, described earlier, is crucial to preventing harm from emerging hazards as the work proceeds. If the task is of any substantial length, many things can change considerably from what they were pre-task. The weather, lighting conditions, adjacent work crews, and workers' physical states are just a few very dynamic factors that could pose emerging safety hazards. Re-scanning needs special focus from management because it is often a weaker behavior than pre-task scanning despite the steps being identical. Several factors can inhibit needed re-scanning:

- The focus on the work task itself may give the workers "tunnel vision" and keep them from seeing emerging hazards in the environment.

- As work on the task nears completion, momentum to plow ahead to reach the end may make pausing to scan less likely than earlier in the task. In aviation, this phenomenon is known as "get-thereitis" and has been noted as sometimes contributing to aircraft crashes.

- There is a clear trigger stimulus for a pretask scan—you're about to start a new task—but the stimulus for a re-scan is less clear. For example, suppose one of your coworkers seems to be getting fatigued as the task proceeds. When do you call for a re-scan? The threshold for an emerging hazard to be seen as a threat is "when safety conditions change" and that is not a crystal-clear criterion.

The best way to teach that threshold is not through attempts to verbally define it, but through discussion of examples and nonexamples with workers to promote community learning. Supervisors might find questions such as, "What changes did you see during the task that might have posed a safety risk, and what did you decide to do about them?" useful to help everyone learn what kinds of situations should trigger rescans and which should not. It's best to lean toward re-scanning if in doubt. It is always safer to re-scan when not needed than to fail to re-scan when it was needed.

Managers can have coaching interactions with frontline supervisors to build and maintain their good coaching skills in a "cascaded coaching" process. ADI's Safety Leadership model is designed to build cascaded coaching and accountability across management levels to strengthen various safety-critical behaviors such as doing effective safety scans. Companies trying to improve their safety culture would benefit from adding safety scans to their safe work procedures and engaging management to make them meaningful tools in use.

---

[1] Endsley, M.R. (1995). "Toward a theory of situation awareness in dynamic situations." *Human Factors*, 37, 65-84. DOI:10.1518/001872095779049543

Killingsworth, K., Miller, S.A., & Alavosius, M.P. (2016). "A behavioral interpretation of situation awareness: Prospects for Organizational Behavior Management." *Journal of Organizational Behavior Management*, 36:4, 301-321. DOI:10.1080/01608061.2016.1236056

[2] Agnew, J., (2016). *A Supervisor's Guide to (Safety) Leadership*. Performance Management Publications.

This article originally appeared on https://www.aubreydaniels.com/media-center/making-safety-hazard-scans-realtime-habits (updated 2021).

APPENDIX TWO

SUGGESTED READINGS

BOOKS

Agnew, Judy, *A. Supervisor's Guide to (Safety) Leadership*. Atlanta: Performance Management Publications, 2016.

Agnew, Judy, and Daniels, Aubrey C. *Safe by Accident? Take the Luck out of Safety: Leadership Practices that Build a Sustainable Safety Culture*. Atlanta: Performance Management Publications, 2010.

Agnew, Judy, and Snyder, Gail. *Removing Obstacles to Safety*. Atlanta: Performance Management Publications, 2000.

Bailey, Jon, and Burch, Mary. *How to Think Like a Behavior Analyst: Understanding the Science that Can Change Your Life*. New York: Taylor and Francis, 2006.

Daniels, Aubrey C. *Bringing Out the Best in People*. New York: McGraw-Hill, 2000.

Daniels, Aubrey C., and Daniels, James E. *Measure of a Leader*. Atlanta: Performance Management Publications, 2005.

Daniels, Aubrey C. *Other People's Habits: How to Use Positive Reinforcement to Bring Out the Best in People Around You*. New York: McGraw-Hill, 2001.

Daniels, Aubrey C. and Bailey, Jon S. *Performance Management: Changing Behavior that Drives Organizational Effectiveness*. Atlanta, GA: Performance Management Publications, 2014.

Dekker, S. *Just Culture: Balancing Safety and Accountability*. Burlington, VT: Ashgate Publishing Company, 2007.

Gilbert, Thomas F. *Human Competence; Engineering Worthy Performance*. San Francisco: Pfeiffer, an imprint of Wiley, 2007.

Latham, Glenn. *The Power of Positive Parenting*. UT: P&T Ink, 1990.

Maloney, Michael. *Teach Your Children Well.* MA: QLC Educational Services, Cambridge Center of Behavioral Studies, 1998.

Pierce, W. David, and Epling, W. Frank. *Behavior Analysis and Learning.* NJ: Pearson Education, 1998.

Reason, J.T. *Managing the Risks of Organizational Accidents.* Burlington, VT: Ashgate Publishing Company, 1997.

Rummler, G.A., and Brache, A.P. *Improving Performance: How to Manage the White Space on the Organization Chart.* San Francisco: Jossey-Bass Publishers, 1995.

Sidman, Murray. *Tactics of Scientific Research.* Boston: Authors Cooperative, 1960.

Sidman, Murray. *Coercion and Its Fallout.* Boston: Authors Cooperative, 1989.

Skinner, B. F. *About Behaviorism.* New York: Knopf, 1974.

Skinner, B. F. *Science and Human Behavior.* New York: The Free Press: MacMillan, 1974.

Skinner, B. F. *Technology of Teaching.* New York: AppletonCenturyCrofts, 1968.

Wetherbee, J. (2017). *Controlling risk in a dangerous world: 30 techniques for operating excellence.* New York: Morgan James.

ARTICLES

Binder, C. (1996). "Behavioral fluency: Evolution of a new paradigm." *The Behavior Analyst,* 19, 163-197.

Curry, S., Gravina, N., Sleiman, A., & Richard, E. (2019). "The effects of engaging in rapport-building behaviors on productivity and discretionary effort." *Journal of Organizational Behavior Management,* 39, 213-226. https://doi.org/10.1080/01608061.2019.1667940.

Ericsson, A. "The Role of Deliberate Practice in the Acquisition of Expert Performance." *Psychological Review.* 3 (1993): 364.

Hallowell, M., Quashne, M., Salas, R., Jones, M., MacLean, B., Quinn, E. (2021). "The Statistical Invalidity of TRIR as a Measure of Safety Performance." *PSJ Professional Safety,* April 2021, 28-34.

Kelley, D., & Gravina, N. (2018). "Every minute counts: Using process improvement and performance feedback to improve patient flow in an emergency department." *Journal of Organizational Behavior Management,* 38, 234-243. https://doi.org/10.1080/016 08061.2017.1423150.

Matey, N., Sleiman, A., Nastasi, J., Richard, E., & Gravina, N. (2021). "Varying reactions to feedback and their effects on observer accuracy and attrition." *Journal of Applied Behavior Analysis. Advanced Online Publication.* https://doi.org/ 10.1002/jaba.840.

Olson, R., Thompson, S. V., Elliot, D. L., Hess, J. A., Luther Rhoten, K., Parker, K. N., Wright, R. R., Wipfli, B., Bettencourt, K. M., Buckmaster, A., Marino, M. (2016). "Safety and health support for home care workers: the COMPASS randomized controlled trial." *American Journal of Public Health,* online first August 2016.

JOURNALS & MAGAZINES

The Behavior Analyst. Association of Behavior Analysis International, 550 W. Centre Ave., Portage, MI 490245364 | Phone: (269) 4929310 | Fax: (269) 4929316 | Email: mail@abainternational.org.

Journal of Applied Behavior Analysis [JABA]. Department of Applied Behavioral Science, University of Kansas, Lawrence, KS 660452133.

Journal of Organizational Behavior Management [JOBM]. Philadelphia: Haworth Press, haworthpress@taylorandfrancis.com.

SAFETY SYSTEMS SERVICES FROM ADI

Aubrey Daniels International improves your safety performance by ensuring all organizational systems support safe work habits.

Despite good intentions, many organizational systems fail to produce desired outcomes and can even undermine safety performance. A scientific understanding of how systems influence behavior enables adjustments to those systems that lead to sustainable safety improvement.

Safety systems such as hazard identification, near-miss reporting, pre-task risk assessment, and Stop Work Authority are essential for promoting safe work but making sure those systems are used effectively is essential for success. Equally important is assessing the complex intersection of non-safety organizational systems on safety-related behavior. Production incentives, quality programs, and other Key Performance Indicators all have the potential to influence safety in unplanned and undesired ways.

ADI offers a systematic approach to designing or redesigning safety and non-safety systems to ensure they have the intended impact on safety performance and safety culture.

Contact ADI to learn more about our approach and how we can help your organization be **safe by design.**

678-904-6140
info@aubreydaniels.com
www.aubreydaniels.com/safety-systems

ABOUT AUBREY DANIELS INTERNATIONAL

Regardless of industry, your people fuel your business. Aubrey Daniels International (ADI) helps clients create an energized and engaged workforce aligned and focused on the behaviors that drive critical business results. We prepare leaders to proactively manage performance in ways consistent with your organization's core values and business objectives.

Our approach—proven in great companies worldwide—is founded on the science of behavior and is refined through four decades of experience developing practical improvement strategies. Our streamlined coaching and leadership accountability process ensures that leaders motivate discretionary effort and optimize business outcomes, workplace culture, and safety performance. When you become an ADI client we customize our approach, meeting you where you are while identifying actionable steps for improvement, then accelerating your path to success and transferring our behavioral expertise to you, ensuring lasting change.

ADI's broad range of consulting support includes:

Safety Solutions

- Safety Leadership
- Training & Coaching
- Safety Systems Improvement
- Behavior-Based Safety

Surveys & Assessments

- Culture
- Leadership
- Process Implementation
- BBS Readiness & Health Check
- Performance & Safety Systems

Behavioral Leadership Solutions

Positive Accountability

Culture Change

Employee Engagement

Strategy Execution

Training & Certification

Let ADI help you create and sustain a positive, safe, and healthy workplace.

www.aubreydaniels.com

OTHER BOOKS YOU'LL LOVE

 Safe by Accident
Aubrey C. Daniels
Judy Agnew

 A Supervisor's Guide to (Safety) Leadership
Judy Agnew

 Removing Obstacles to Safety
Judy Agnew
Gail Snyder

 Bringing Out the Best in People
Aubrey C. Daniels

 Other People's Habits
Aubrey C. Daniels

 ***Measure of a Leader***
Aubrey C. Daniels
James E. Daniels

 ***Performance Management***
Aubrey C. Daniels
Jon S. Bailey

 ***OOPS!***
Aubrey C. Daniels

Visit our online store at www.aubreydaniels.com/store

ABOUT THE AUTHORS

Judy Agnew

Senior Vice President, Safety Solutions
Aubrey Daniels International

Judy Agnew, Ph.D., is a seasoned consultant, trusted advisor, and recognized thought leader in workplace safety and safety leadership. Agnew partners with clients to create evidence-based interventions that are safe by design and result in optimal and sustainable organizational change. With more than 30 years of consulting experience, Agnew successfully works with diverse employee populations across a wide range of organizational issues, helping clients achieve targeted performance objectives.

Agnew is an active speaker and invited presenter at major national and international safety conferences and corporate events. She is frequently interviewed for national and trade publications and is the author of three other highly-regarded safety books: *Removing Obstacles to Safety* (with Gail Snyder), *Safe by Accident? Leadership Practices that Build a Sustainable Safety Culture* (with Aubrey Daniels), and *A Supervisor's Guide to (Safety) Leadership*.

ABOUT THE AUTHORS

David Uhl

Senior Vice President, Consulting Services
Aubrey Daniels International

David Uhl is a results-driven consultant with a track record of success working at every organizational level. Uhl is known for his flexibility and adaptability, helping his clients in aerospace, energy, mining, manufacturing, healthcare, financial services, and customer care; to maximize the discretionary effort of their employees. With over 25 years of experience, Uhl is a seasoned executive coach, change leader, and master facilitator who is adept at applying behavioral science technology to accelerate and sustain organizational change and performance improvement.

Uhl has been a returning faculty member for The Institute of Nuclear Power Operations (INPO) since 2001 and is a frequent conference presenter. Uhl is requested to deliver sessions that address leadership and organizational challenges, particularly those relating to high-hazard environments or the rapid execution of organizational change.